EVERY MAN OUT OF HIS HUMOUR

TO THE
NOBLEST NURSERIES OF HUMANITY AND
LIBERTY IN THE KINGDOM

INTRODUCTION

THE greatest of English dramatists except Shakespeare, the first literary dictator and poet-laureate, a writer of verse, prose, satire, and criticism who most potently of all the men of his time affected the subsequent course of English letters: such was Ben Jonson, and as such his strong personality assumes an interest to us almost unparalleled, at least in his age.

Ben Jonson came of the stock that was centuries after to give to the world Thomas Carlyle; for Jonson's grandfather was of Annandale, over the Solway, whence he migrated to England. Jonson's father lost his estate under Queen Mary, "having been cast into prison and forfeited." He entered the church, but died a month before his illustrious son was born, leaving his widow and child in poverty. Jonson's birthplace was Westminster, and the time of his birth early in 1573. He was thus nearly ten years Shakespeare's junior, and less well off, if a trifle better born. But Jonson did not profit even by this slight advantage. His mother married beneath her, a wright or bricklayer, and Jonson was for a time apprenticed to the trade. As a youth he attracted the attention of the famous antiquary, William Camden, then usher at Westminster School, and there the poet laid the solid foundations of his classical learning. Jonson always held Camden in veneration, acknowledging that to him he owed, "All that I am in arts, all that I know:" and dedicating his first dramatic success, "Every Man in His Humour," to him. It is doubtful whether Jonson ever went to either university, though Fuller says that he was "statutably admitted into St. John's College, Cambridge." He tells us that he took no degree, but was later "Master of Arts in both the universities, by their favour, not his study." When a mere youth Jonson enlisted as a soldier trailing his pike in Flanders in the protracted wars of William the Silent against the Spanish. Jonson was a large and rawboned lad; he became by his own account in time exceedingly bulky. In chat with his friend William Drummond of Hawthornden, Jonson told how "in his service in the Low Countries he had, in the face of both the camps, killed an enemy, and taken 'opima spolia' from him;" and how "since his coming to England, being appealed to the fields, he had killed his adversary which had hurt him in the arm and whose sword was ten inches longer than his." Jonson's reach may have made up for the lack of his sword; certainly his prowess lost nothing in the telling. Obviously Jonson was brave, combative, and not averse to talking of himself and his doings.

In 1592, Jonson returned from abroad penniless. Soon after he married, almost as early and quite as imprudently as Shakespeare. He told Drummond curtly that "his wife was a shrew, yet honest"; for some years he lived apart from her in the household of Lord Albany. Yet two touching epitaphs among Jonson's 'Epigrams', "On my first daughter," and "On my first son," attest the warmth of the poet's family affections. The daughter died in infancy, the son of the plague; another son grew up to manhood little credit to his father whom he survived. We know nothing beyond this of Jonson's domestic life.

How soon Jonson drifted into what we now call grandly "the theatrical profession" we do not know. In 1593 Marlowe made his tragic exit from life, and Greene, Shakespeare's other rival on the popular stage, had preceded Marlowe in an equally miserable death the year before. Shakespeare already had the running to himself. Jonson appears first in the employment of Philip Henslowe, the exploiter of several troupes of players, manager, and father-in-law of the famous actor, Edward Alleyn. From entries in 'Henslowe's Diary', a species of theatrical account book which has been handed down to us, we know that Jonson was connected with the Admiral's men; for he borrowed £4 of Henslowe, July 28, 1597, paying back 3s. 9d. on the same day on account of his "share" (in what is not altogether clear); while later, on December 3, of the same year, Henslowe advanced 20s. to him "upon a book which he showed the plot unto the company which he promised to deliver unto the company at Christmas next." In the next August Jonson was in collaboration with Chettle and Porter in a play called "Hot Anger Soon Cold." All this points to an association with Henslowe of some duration, as no mere tyro would be thus paid in advance upon mere promise. From allusions in Dekker's play, "Satiromastix," it appears that Jonson, like Shakespeare, began life as an actor, and that he "ambled in a leather pitch by a play-wagon" taking at one time the part of Hieronimo in Kyd's famous play, "The Spanish Tragedy." By the beginning of 1598, Jonson, though still in needy circumstances, had begun to receive recognition. Francis Meres—well known for his "Comparative Discourse of our English Poets with the Greek, Latin, and Italian Poets," printed in 1598, and for his mention therein of a dozen plays of Shakespeare by title—accords to Ben Jonson a place as one of "our best in tragedy," a matter of some surprise, as no known tragedy of Jonson from so early a date has come down to us. That Jonson was at work on tragedy, however, is proved by the entries in Henslowe of at least three tragedies, now lost, in which he had a hand. These are "Page of Plymouth," "King Robert II. of Scotland," and "Richard Crookback." But all of these came later, on his return to Henslowe, and range from August 1599 to June 1602.

Returning to the autumn of 1598, an event now happened to sever for a time Jonson's relations with Henslowe. In a letter to Alleyn, dated September 26 of that year, Henslowe writes: "I have lost one of my company that hurteth me greatly; that is Gabriel [Spencer], for he is slain in Hogsden fields by the hands of Benjamin Jonson, bricklayer." The last word is perhaps Henslowe's thrust at Jonson in his displeasure rather than a designation of his actual continuance at his trade up to this time. It is fair to Jonson to remark however, that his adversary appears to have been a notorious fire-eater who had shortly before killed one Feeke in a similar squabble. Duelling was a frequent occurrence of the time among gentlemen and the nobility; it was an imprudent breach of the peace on the part of a player. This duel is the one which Jonson described years after to Drummond, and for it Jonson was duly arraigned at Old Bailey, tried, and convicted. He was sent to prison and such goods and chattels as he had "were forfeited." It is a thought to give one pause that, but for the ancient law permitting convicted felons to plead, as it was called, the benefit of clergy, Jonson might have been hanged for this deed. The circumstance that the poet could read and write saved him; and he received only a brand of the letter "T," for Tyburn, on his left thumb. While in jail Jonson became a Roman Catholic; but he returned to the faith of the Church of England a dozen years later.

On his release, in disgrace with Henslowe and his former associates, Jonson offered his services as a playwright to Henslowe's rivals, the Lord Chamberlain's company, in which Shakespeare was a prominent shareholder. A tradition of long standing, though not susceptible of proof in a court of law, narrates that Jonson had submitted the manuscript of "Every Man in His Humour" to the Chamberlain's men and had received from the company a refusal; that Shakespeare called him back, read the play himself, and at once accepted it. Whether this story is true or not, certain it is that "Every Man in His Humour" was accepted by Shakespeare's company and acted for the first time in 1598, with Shakespeare taking a part. The evidence of this is contained in the list of actors prefixed to the comedy in the folio of Jonson's works, 1616. But it is a mistake to infer, because Shakespeare's name stands first in the list of actors and the elder Kno'well first in the 'dramatis personae', that Shakespeare took that particular part. The order of a list of Elizabethan players was generally that of their importance or priority as shareholders in the company and seldom if ever corresponded to the list of characters.

"Every Man in His Humour" was an immediate success, and with it Jonson's reputation as one of the leading dramatists of his time was established once and for all. This could have been by no means Jonson's earliest comedy, and we have just learned that he was already reputed one

12

of "our best in tragedy." Indeed, one of Jonson's extant comedies, "The Case is Altered," but one never claimed by him or published as his, must certainly have preceded "Every Man in His Humour" on the stage. The former play may be described as a comedy modelled on the Latin plays of Plautus. (It combines, in fact, situations derived from the "Captivi" and the "Aulularia" of that dramatist). But the pretty story of the beggar-maiden, Rachel, and her suitors, Jonson found, not among the classics, but in the ideals of romantic love which Shakespeare had already popularised on the stage. Jonson never again produced so fresh and lovable a feminine personage as Rachel, although in other respects "The Case is Altered" is not a conspicuous play, and, save for the satirising of Antony Munday in the person of Antonio Balladino and Gabriel Harvey as well, is perhaps the least characteristic of the comedies of Jonson.

"Every Man in His Humour," probably first acted late in the summer of 1598 and at the Curtain, is commonly regarded as an epoch-making play; and this view is not unjustified. As to plot, it tells little more than how an intercepted letter enabled a father to follow his supposedly studious son to London, and there observe his life with the gallants of the time. The real quality of this comedy is in its personages and in the theory upon which they are conceived. Ben Jonson had theories about poetry and the drama, and he was neither chary in talking of them nor in experimenting with them in his plays. This makes Jonson, like Dryden in his time, and Wordsworth much later, an author to reckon with; particularly when we remember that many of Jonson's notions came for a time definitely to prevail and to modify the whole trend of English poetry. First of all Jonson was a classicist, that is, he believed in restraint and precedent in art in opposition to the prevalent ungoverned and irresponsible Renaissance spirit. Jonson believed that there was a professional way of doing things which might be reached by a study of the best examples, and he found these examples for the most part among the ancients. To confine our attention to the drama, Jonson objected to the amateurishness and haphazard nature of many contemporary plays, and set himself to do something different; and the first and most striking thing that he evolved was his conception and practice of the comedy of humours.

As Jonson has been much misrepresented in this matter, let us quote his own words as to "humour." A humour, according to Jonson, was a bias of disposition, a warp, so to speak, in character by which

"Some one peculiar quality
Doth so possess a man, that it doth draw
All his affects, his spirits, and his powers,
In their confluctions, all to run one way."

But continuing, Jonson is careful to add:
"But that a rook by wearing a pied feather,
The cable hat-band, or the three-piled ruff,
A yard of shoe-tie, or the Switzers knot
On his French garters, should affect a humour!
O, it is more than most ridiculous."

Jonson's comedy of humours, in a word, conceived of stage personages on the basis of a ruling trait or passion (a notable simplification of actual life be it observed in passing); and, placing these typified traits in juxtaposition in their conflict and contrast, struck the spark of comedy. Downright, as his name indicates, is "a plain squire"; Bobadill's humour is that of the braggart who is incidentally, and with delightfully comic effect, a coward; Brainworm's humour is the finding out of things to the end of fooling everybody: of course he is fooled in the end himself. But it was not Jonson's theories alone that made the success of "Every Man in His Humour." The play is admirably written and each character is vividly conceived, and with a firm touch based on observation of the men of the London of the day. Jonson was neither in this, his first great comedy (nor in any other play that he wrote), a supine classicist, urging that English drama return to a slavish adherence to classical conditions.

14

He says as to the laws of the old comedy (meaning by "laws," such matters as the unities of time and place and the use of chorus): "I see not then, but we should enjoy the same licence, or free power to illustrate and heighten our invention as they [the ancients] did; and not be tied to those strict and regular forms which the niceness of a few, who are nothing but form, would thrust upon us." "Every Man in His Humour" is written in prose, a novel practice which Jonson had of his predecessor in comedy, John Lyly. Even the word "humour" seems to have been employed in the Jonsonian sense by Chapman before Jonson's use of it. Indeed, the comedy of humours itself is only a heightened variety of the comedy of manners which represents life, viewed at a satirical angle, and is the oldest and most persistent species of comedy in the language. None the less, Jonson's comedy merited its immediate success and marked out a definite course in which comedy long continued to run. To mention only Shakespeare's Falstaff and his rout, Bardolph, Pistol, Dame Quickly, and the rest, whether in "Henry IV." or in "The Merry Wives of Windsor," all are conceived in the spirit of humours. So are the captains, Welsh, Scotch, and Irish of "Henry V.," and Malvolio especially later; though Shakespeare never employed the method of humours for an important personage. It was not Jonson's fault that many of his successors did precisely the thing that he had reprobated, that is, degrade "the humour: into an oddity of speech, an eccentricity of manner, of dress, or cut of beard. There was an anonymous play called "Every Woman in Her Humour." Chapman wrote "A Humourous Day's Mirth," Day, "Humour Out of Breath," Fletcher later, "The Humourous Lieutenant," and Jonson, besides "Every Man Out of His Humour," returned to the title in closing the cycle of his comedies in "The Magnetic Lady or Humours Reconciled."

With the performance of "Every Man Out of His Humour" in 1599, by Shakespeare's company once more at the Globe, we turn a new page in Jonson's career. Despite his many real virtues, if there is one feature more than any other that distinguishes Jonson, it is his arrogance; and to this may be added his self-righteousness, especially under criticism or satire.

15

"Every Man Out of His Humour" is the first of three "comical satires" which Jonson contributed to what Dekker called the 'poetomachia' or war of the theatres as recent critics have named it. This play as a fabric of plot is a very slight affair; but as a satirical picture of the manners of the time, proceeding by means of vivid caricature, couched in witty and brilliant dialogue and sustained by that righteous indignation which must lie at the heart of all true satire—as a realisation, in short, of the classical ideal of comedy—there had been nothing like Jonson's comedy since the days of Aristophanes. "Every Man in His Humour," like the two plays that follow it, contains two kinds of attack, the critical or generally satiric, levelled at abuses and corruptions in the abstract; and the personal, in which specific application is made of all this in the lampooning of poets and others, Jonson's contemporaries. The method of personal attack by actual caricature of a person on the stage is almost as old as the drama. Aristophanes so lampooned Euripides in "The Acharnians" and Socrates in "The Clouds," to mention no other examples; and in English drama this kind of thing is alluded to again and again. What Jonson really did, was to raise the dramatic lampoon to an art, and make out of a casual burlesque and bit of mimicry a dramatic satire of literary pretensions and permanency. With the arrogant attitude mentioned above and his uncommon eloquence in scorn, vituperation, and invective, it is no wonder that Jonson soon involved himself in literary and even personal quarrels with his fellow-authors. The circumstances of the origin of this 'poetomachia' are far from clear, and those who have written on the topic, except of late, have not helped to make them clearer. The origin of the "war" has been referred to satirical references, apparently to Jonson, contained in "The Scourge of Villainy," a satire in regular form after the manner of the ancients by John Marston, a fellow playwright, subsequent friend and collaborator of Jonson's. On the other hand, epigrams of Jonson have been discovered (49, 68, and 100) variously charging "playwright" (reasonably identified with Marston) with scurrility, cowardice, and plagiarism; though the dates of the epigrams cannot be ascertained with certainty. Jonson's own statement of the matter to Drummond runs: "He had many quarrels with Marston, beat him, and took his pistol from him, wrote his 'Poetaster' on him; the beginning[s] of them were that Marston represented him on the stage."[1]

Here at least we are on certain ground; and the principals of the quarrel are known. "Histriomastix," a play revised by Marston in 1598, has been regarded as the one in which Jonson was thus "represented on the stage"; although the personage in question, Chrisogonus, a poet, satirist, and translator, poor but proud, and contemptuous of the common herd, seems rather a complimentary portrait of Jonson than a caricature. As to the personages actually ridiculed in "Every Man Out of His Humour," Carlo Buffone was formerly thought certainly to be Marston, as he was described as "a public scurrilous, and profane jester," and elsewhere as the grand scourge or second untruss [that is, satirist], of the time" (Joseph Hall being by his own boast the first, and Marston's work being entitled "The Scourge of Villainy"). Apparently we must now prefer for Carlo a notorious character named Charles Chester, of whom gossipy and inaccurate Aubrey relates that he was "a bold impertinent fellow . . . a perpetual talker and made a noise like a drum in a room. So one time at a tavern Sir Walter Raleigh beats him and seals up his mouth (that is his upper and nether beard) with hard wax. From him Ben Jonson takes his Carlo Buffone ['i.e.', jester] in 'Every Man in His Humour'." Is it conceivable that after all Jonson was ridiculing Marston, and that the point of the satire consisted in an intentional confusion of "the grand scourge or second untruss" with "the scurrilous and profane" Chester?

We have digressed into detail in this particular case to exemplify the difficulties of criticism in its attempts to identify the allusions in these

---

1   The best account of this whole subject is to be found in the edition of 'Poetaster' and 'Satiromastix' by J. H. Penniman in 'Belles Lettres Series' shortly to appear. See also his earlier work, 'The War of the Theatres', 1892, and the excellent contributions to the subject by H. C. Hart in 'Notes and Queries', and in his edition of Jonson, 1906.

forgotten quarrels. We are on sounder ground of fact in recording other manifestations of Jonson's enmity. In "The Case is Altered" there is clear ridicule in the character Antonio Balladino of Anthony Munday, pageant-poet of the city, translator of romances and playwright as well. In "Every Man in His Humour" there is certainly a caricature of Samuel Daniel, accepted poet of the court, sonneteer, and companion of men of fashion. These men held recognised positions to which Jonson felt his talents better entitled him; they were hence to him his natural enemies. It seems almost certain that he pursued both in the personages of his satire through "Every Man Out of His Humour," and "Cynthia's Revels," Daniel under the characters Fastidious Brisk and Hedon, Munday as Puntarvolo and Amorphus; but in these last we venture on quagmire once more. Jonson's literary rivalry of Daniel is traceable again and again, in the entertainments that welcomed King James on his way to London, in the masques at court, and in the pastoral drama. As to Jonson's personal ambitions with respect to these two men, it is notable that he became, not pageant-poet, but chronologer to the City of London; and that, on the accession of the new king, he came soon to triumph over Daniel as the accepted entertainer of royalty.

"Cynthia's Revels," the second "comical satire," was acted in 1600, and, as a play, is even more lengthy, elaborate, and impossible than "Every Man Out of His Humour." Here personal satire seems to have absorbed everything, and while much of the caricature is admirable, especially in the detail of witty and trenchantly satirical dialogue, the central idea of a fountain of self-love is not very well carried out, and the persons revert at times to abstractions, the action to allegory. It adds to our wonder that this difficult drama should have been acted by the Children of Queen Elizabeth's Chapel, among them Nathaniel Field with whom Jonson read Horace and Martial, and whom he taught later how to make plays. Another of these precocious little actors was Salathiel Pavy, who died before he was thirteen, already famed for taking the parts of old men. Him Jonson immortalised in one of the sweetest of his epitaphs. An interesting sidelight is this on the character of this redoubtable and rugged satirist, that he should thus have befriended and tenderly remembered these little theatrical waifs, some of whom (as we know) had been literally kidnapped to be pressed into the service of the theatre and whipped to the conning of their difficult parts. To the caricature of Daniel and Munday in "Cynthia's Revels" must be added Anaides (impudence), here assuredly Marston, and Asotus (the prodigal), interpreted as Lodge or, more perilously, Raleigh. Crites, like Asper-Macilente in "Every Man Out of His Humour," is Jonson's self-complaisant portrait of himself, the just, wholly admirable, and judicious scholar, holding his head high above the pack of the yelping curs of envy and detraction, but careless of their puny attacks on his perfections with only too mindful a neglect.

The third and last of the "comical satires" is "Poetaster," acted, once more, by the Children of the Chapel in 1601, and Jonson's only avowed contribution to the fray. According to the author's own account, this play was written in fifteen weeks on a report that his enemies had entrusted to Dekker the preparation of "Satiromastix, the Untrussing of the Humorous Poet," a dramatic attack upon himself. In this attempt to forestall his enemies Jonson succeeded, and "Poetaster" was an immediate and deserved success. While hardly more closely knit in structure than its earlier companion pieces, "Poetaster" is planned to lead up to the ludicrous final scene in which, after a device borrowed from the "Lexiphanes" of Lucian, the offending poetaster, Marston-Crispinus, is made to throw up the difficult words with which he had overburdened his stomach as well as overlarded his vocabulary. In the end Crispinus with his fellow, Dekker-Demetrius, is bound over to keep the peace and never thenceforward "malign, traduce, or detract the person or writings of Quintus Horatius Flaccus [Jonson] or any other eminent man transcending you in merit." One of the most diverting personages in Jonson's comedy is Captain Tucca. "His peculiarity" has been well described by Ward as "a buoyant blackguardism which recovers itself instantaneously from the most complete exposure, and a picturesqueness of speech like that of a walking dictionary of slang."

It was this character, Captain Tucca, that Dekker hit upon in his reply, "Satiromastix," and he amplified him, turning his abusive vocabulary back upon Jonson and adding "An immodesty to his dialogue that did not enter into Jonson's conception." It has been held, altogether plausibly, that when Dekker was engaged professionally, so to speak, to write a dramatic reply to Jonson, he was at work on a species of chronicle history, dealing with the story of Walter Terill in the reign of William Rufus. This he hurriedly adapted to include the satirical characters suggested by "Poetaster," and fashioned to convey the satire of his reply. The absurdity of placing Horace in the court of a Norman king is the result. But Dekker's play is not without its palpable hits at the arrogance, the literary pride, and self-righteousness of Jonson-Horace, whose "ningle" or pal, the absurd Asinius Bubo, has recently been shown to figure forth, in all likelihood, Jonson's friend, the poet Drayton. Slight and hastily adapted as is "Satiromastix," especially in a comparison with the better wrought and more significant satire of "Poetaster," the town awarded the palm to Dekker, not to Jonson; and Jonson gave over in consequence his practice of "comical satire." Though Jonson was cited to appear before the Lord Chief Justice to answer certain charges to the effect that he had attacked lawyers and soldiers in "Poetaster," nothing came of this complaint. It may be suspected that much of this furious clatter and give-and-take was pure playing to the gallery. The town was agog with the strife, and on no less an authority than Shakespeare ("Hamlet," ii. 2), we learn that the children's company (acting the plays of Jonson) did "so berattle the common stages . . . that many, wearing rapiers, are afraid of goose-quills, and dare scarce come thither."

Several other plays have been thought to bear a greater or less part in the war of the theatres. Among them the most important is a college play, entitled "The Return from Parnassus," dating 1601-02. In it a much-quoted passage makes Burbage, as a character, declare: "Why here's our fellow Shakespeare puts them all down; aye and Ben Jonson, too. O that Ben Jonson is a pestilent fellow; he brought up Horace, giving the poets a pill, but our fellow Shakespeare hath given him a purge that made him bewray his credit." Was Shakespeare then concerned in this war of the stages? And what could have been the nature of this "purge"? Among several suggestions, "Troilus and Cressida" has been thought by some to be the play in which Shakespeare thus "put down" his friend, Jonson. A wiser interpretation finds the "purge" in "Satiromastix," which, though not .written by Shakespeare, was staged by his company, and therefore with his approval and under his direction as one of the leaders of that company.

The last years of the reign of Elizabeth thus saw Jonson recognised as a dramatist second only to Shakespeare, and not second even to him as a dramatic satirist. But Jonson now turned his talents to new fields. Plays on subjects derived from classical story and myth had held the stage from the beginning of the drama, so that Shakespeare was making no new departure when he wrote his "Julius Caesar" about 1600. Therefore when Jonson staged "Sejanus," three years later and with Shakespeare'scompany once more, he was only following in the elder dramatist's footsteps. But Jonson's idea of a play on classical history, on the one hand, and Shakespeare's and the elder popular dramatists, on the other, were very different. Heywood some years before had put five straggling plays on the stage in quick succession, all derived from stories in Ovid and dramatised with little taste or discrimination. Shakespeare had a finer conception of form, but even he was contented to take all his ancient history from North's translation of Plutarch and dramatise his subject without further inquiry. Jonson was a scholar and a classical antiquarian. He reprobated this slipshod amateurishness, and wrote his "Sejanus" like a scholar, reading Tacitus, Suetonius, and other authorities, to be certain of his facts, his setting, and his atmosphere, and somewhat pedantically noting his authorities in the margin when he came to print. "Sejanus" is a tragedy of genuine dramatic power in which is told with discriminating taste the story of the haughty favourite of Tiberius with his tragical overthrow. Our drama presents no truer nor more painstaking representation of ancient Roman life than may be found in Jonson's "Sejanus" and "Catiline his Conspiracy," which followed in 1611. A passage in the address of the former play to the reader, in which Jonson refers to a collaboration in an earlier version, has led to the surmise that Shakespeare may have been that "worthier pen." There is no evidence to determine the matter.

In 1605, we find Jonson in active collaboration with Chapman and Marston in the admirable comedy of London life entitled "Eastward Hoe." In the previous year, Marston had dedicated his "Malcontent," in terms of fervid admiration, to Jonson; so that the wounds of the war of the theatres must have been long since healed. Between Jonson and Chapman there was the kinship of similar scholarly ideals. The two continued friends throughout life. "Eastward Hoe" achieved the extraordinary popularity represented in a demand for three issues in one year. But this was not due entirely to the merits of the play. In its earliest version a passage which an irritable courtier conceived to be derogatory to his nation, the Scots, sent both Chapman and Jonson to jail; but the matter was soon patched up, for by this time Jonson had influence at court.

With the accession of King James, Jonson began his long and successful career as a writer of masques. He wrote more masques than all his competitors together, and they are of an extraordinary variety and poetic excellence. Jonson did not invent the masque; for such premeditated devices to set and frame, so to speak, a court ball had been known and practised in varying degrees of elaboration long before his time. But Jonson gave dramatic value to the masque, especially in his invention of the antimasque, a comedy or farcical element of relief, entrusted to professional players or dancers. He enhanced, as well, the beauty and dignity of those portions of the masque in which noble lords and ladies took their parts to create, by their gorgeous costumes and artistic grouping and evolutions, a sumptuous show. On the mechanical and scenic side Jonson had an inventive and ingenious partner in Inigo Jones, the royal architect, who more than any one man raised the standard of stage representation in the England of his day. Jonson continued active in the service of the court in the writing of masques and other entertainments far into the reign of King Charles; but, towards the end, a quarrel with Jones embittered his life, and the two testy old men appear to have become not only a constant irritation to each other, but intolerable bores at court. In "Hymenaei," "The Masque of Queens," "Love Freed from Ignorance," "Lovers made Men," "Pleasure Reconciled to Virtue," and many more will be found Jonson's aptitude, his taste, his poetry and inventiveness in these by-forms of the drama; while in "The Masque of Christmas," and "The Gipsies Metamorphosed" especially, is discoverable that power of broad comedy which, at court as well as in the city, was not the least element of Jonson's contemporary popularity.

But Jonson had by no means given up the popular stage when he turned to the amusement of King James. In 1605 "Volpone" was produced, "The Silent Woman" in 1609, "The Alchemist" in the following year. These comedies, with "Bartholomew Fair," 1614, represent Jonson at his height, and for constructive cleverness, character successfully conceived in the manner of caricature, wit and brilliancy of dialogue, they stand alone in English drama. "Volpone, or the Fox," is, in a sense, a transition play from the dramatic satires of the war of the theatres to the purer comedy represented in the plays named above. Its subject is a struggle of wit applied to chicanery; for among its 'dramatis personae', from the villainous Fox himself, his rascally servant Mosca, Voltore (the vulture), Corbaccio and Corvino (the big and the little raven), to Sir Politic Would-be and the rest, there is scarcely a virtuous character in the play. Question has been raised as to whether a story so forbidding can be considered a comedy, for, although the plot ends in the discomfiture and impriso`nment of the most vicious, it involves no moral catastrophe. But Jonson was on sound historical ground, for "Volpone" is conceived far more logically on the lines of the ancients' theory of comedy than was ever the romantic drama of Shakespeare, however repulsive we may find a philosophy of life that facilely divides the world into the rogues and their dupes, and, identifying brains with roguery and innocence with folly, admires the former while inconsistently punishing them.

"The Silent Woman" is a gigantic farce of the most ingenious construction. The whole comedy hinges on a huge joke, played by a heartless nephew on his misanthropic uncle, who is induced to take to himself a wife, young, fair, and warranted silent, but who, in the end, turns out neither silent nor a woman at all. In "The Alchemist," again, we have the utmost cleverness in construction, the whole fabric building climax on climax, witty, ingenious, and so plausibly presented that we forget its departures from the possibilities of life. In "The Alchemist" Jonson represented, none the less to the life, certain sharpers of the metropolis, revelling in their shrewdness and rascality and in the variety of the stupidity and wickedness of their victims. We may object to the fact that the only person in the play possessed of a scruple of honesty is discomfited, and that the greatest scoundrel of all is approved in the end and rewarded. The comedy is so admirably written and contrived, the personages stand out with such lifelike distinctness in their several kinds, and the whole is animated with such verve and resourcefulness that "The Alchemist" is a new marvel every time it is read. Lastly of this group comes the tremendous comedy, "Bartholomew Fair," less clear cut, less definite, and less structurally worthy of praise than its three predecessors, but full of the keenest and cleverest of satire and inventive to a degree beyond any English comedy save some other of Jonson's own. It is in "Bartholomew Fair" that we are presented to the immortal caricature of the Puritan, Zeal-in-the-Land Busy, and the Littlewits that group about him, and it is in this extraordinary comedy that the humour of Jonson, always open to this danger, loosens into the Rabelaisian mode that so delighted King James in "The Gipsies Metamorphosed." Another comedy of less merit is "The Devil is an Ass," acted in 1616. It was the failure of this play that caused Jonson to give over writing for the public stage for a period of nearly ten years.

"Volpone" was laid as to scene in Venice. Whether because of the success of "Eastward Hoe" or for other reasons, the other three comedies declare in the words of the prologue to "The Alchemist": "Our scene is London, 'cause we would make known No country's mirth is better than our own." Indeed Jonson went further when he came to revise his plays for collected publication in his folio of 1616, he transferred the scene of "Every Man in His Humou r" from Florence to London also, converting Signior Lorenzo di Pazzi to Old Kno'well, Prospero to Master Welborn, and Hesperida to Dame Kitely "dwelling i' the Old Jewry."

In his comedies of London life, despite his trend towards caricature, Jonson has shown himself a genuine realist, drawing from the life about him with an experience and insight rare in any generation. A happy comparison has been suggested between Ben Jonson and Charles Dickens. Both were men of the people, lowly born and hardly bred. Each knew the London of his time as few men knew it; and each represented it intimately and in elaborate detail. Both men were at heart moralists, seeking the truth by the exaggerated methods of humour and caricature; perverse, even wrong-headed at times, but possessed of a true pathos and largeness of heart, and when all has been said—though the Elizabethan ran to satire, the Victorian to sentimentality—leaving the world better for the art that they practised in it.

In 1616, the year of the death of Shakespeare, Jonson collected his plays, his poetry, and his masques for publication in a collective edition. This was an unusual thing at the time and had been attempted by no dramatist before Jonson. This volume published, in a carefully revised text, all the plays thus far mentioned, excepting "The Case is Altered," which Jonson did not acknowledge, "Bartholomew Fair," and "The Devil is an Ass," which was written too late. It included likewise a book of some hundred and thirty odd 'Epigrams', in which form of brief and pungent writing Jonson was an acknowledged master; "The Forest," a smaller collection of lyric and occasional verse and some ten 'Masques' and 'Entertainments'. In this same year Jonson was made poet laureate with a pension of one hundred marks a year. This, with his fees and returns from several noblemen, and the small earnings of his plays must have formed the bulk of his income. The poet appears to have done certain literary hack-work for others, as, for example, parts of the Punic Wars contributed to Raleigh's 'History of the World'. We know from a story, little to the credit of either, that Jonson accompanied Raleigh's son abroad in the capacity of a tutor. In 1618 Jonson was granted the reversion of the office of Master of the Revels, a post for which he was peculiarly fitted; but he did not live to enjoy its perquisites. Jonson was honoured with degrees by both universities, though when and under what circumstances is not known. It has been said that he narrowly escaped the honour of knighthood, which the satirists of the day averred King James was wont to lavish with an indiscriminate hand. Worse men were made knights in his day than worthy Ben Jonson.

From 1616 to the close of the reign of King James, Jonson produced nothing for the stage. But he "prosecuted" what he calls "his wonted studies" with such assiduity that he became in reality, as by report, one of the most learned men of his time. Jonson's theory of authorship involved a wide acquaintance with books and "an ability," as he put it, "to convert the substance or riches of another poet to his own use." Accordingly Jonson read not only the Greek and Latin classics down to the lesser writers, but he acquainted himself especially with the Latin writings of his learned contemporaries, their prose as well as their poetry, their antiquities and curious lore as well as their more solid learning. Though a poor man, Jonson was an indefatigable collector of books. He told Drummond that "the Earl of Pembroke sent him £20 every first day of the new year to buy new books." Unhappily, in 1623, his library was destroyed by fire, an accident serio-comically described in his witty poem, "An Execration upon Vulcan." Yet even now a book turns up from time to time in which is inscribed, in fair large Italian lettering, the name, Ben Jonson. With respect to Jonson's use of his material, Dryden said memorably of him: "[He] was not only a professed imitator of Horace, but a learned plagiary of all the others; you track him everywhere in their snow . . . But he has done his robberies so openly that one sees he fears not to be taxed by any law. He invades authors like a monarch, and what would be theft in other poets is only victory in him." And yet it is but fair to say that Jonson prided himself, and justly, on his originality. In "Catiline," he not only uses Sallust's account of the conspiracy, but he models some of the speeches of Cicero on the Roman orator's actual words. In "Poetaster," he lifts a whole satire out of Horace and dramatises it effectively for his purposes. The sophist Libanius suggests the situation of "The Silent Woman"; a Latin comedy of Giordano Bruno, "Il Candelaio," the relation of the dupes and the sharpers in "The Alchemist," the "Mostellaria" of Plautus, its admirable opening scene. But Jonson commonly bettered his sources, and putting the stamp of his sovereignty on whatever bullion he borrowed made it thenceforward to all time current and his own.

The lyric and especially the occasional poetry of Jonson has a peculiar merit. His theory demanded design and the perfection of literary finish. He was furthest from the rhapsodist and the careless singer of an idle day; and he believed that Apollo could only be worthily served in singing robes and laurel crowned. And yet many of Jonson's lyrics will live as long as the language. Who does not know "Queen and huntress, chaste and fair." "Drink to me only with thine eyes," or "Still to be neat, still to be dressed"? Beautiful in form, deft and graceful in expression, with not a word too much or one that bears not its part in the total effect, there is yet about the lyrics of Jonson a certain stiffness and formality, a suspicion that they were not quite spontaneous and unbidden, but that they were carved, so to speak, with disproportionate labour by a potent man of letters whose habitual thought is on greater things. It is for these reasons that Jonson is even better in the epigram and in occasional verse where rhetorical finish and pointed wit less interfere with the spontaneity and emotion which we usually associate with lyrical poetry. There are no

27

such epitaphs as Ben Jonson's, witness the charming ones on his own children, on Salathiel Pavy, the child-actor, and many more; and this even though the rigid law of mine and thine must now restore to William Browne of Tavistock the famous lines beginning: "Underneath this sable hearse." Jonson is unsurpassed, too, in the difficult poetry of compliment, seldom falling into fulsome praise and disproportionate similitude, yet showing again and again a generous appreciation of worth in others, a discriminating taste and a generous personal regard. There was no man in England of his rank so well known and universally beloved as Ben Jonson. The list of his friends, of those to whom he had written verses, and those who had written verses to him, includes the name of every man of prominence in the England of King James. And the tone of many of these productions discloses an affectionate familiarity that speaks for the amiable personality and sound worth of the laureate. In 1619, growing unwieldy through inactivity, Jonson hit upon the heroic remedy of a journey afoot to Scotland. On his way thither and back he was hospitably received at the houses of many friends and by those to whom his friends had recommended him. When he arrived in Edinburgh, the burgesses met to grant him the freedom of the city, and Drummond, foremost of Scottish poets, was proud to entertain him for weeks as his guest at Hawthornden. Some of the noblest of Jonson's poems were inspired by friendship. Such is the fine "Ode to the memory of Sir Lucius Cary and Sir Henry Moryson," and that admirable piece of critical insight and filial affection, prefixed to the first Shakespeare folio, "To the memory of my beloved master, William Shakespeare, and what he hath left us." to mention only these. Nor can the earlier "Epode," beginning "Not to know vice at all," be matchedin stately gravity and gnomic wisdom in its own wise and stately age.

But if Jonson had deserted the stage after the publication of his folio and up to the end of the reign of King James, he was far from inactive; for year after year his inexhaustible inventiveness continued to contribute to the masquing and entertainment at court. In "The Golden

Age Restored," Pallas turns from the Iron Age with its attendant evils into statues which sink out of sight; in "Pleasure Reconciled to Virtue," Atlas figures represented as an old man, his shoulders covered with snow, and Comus, "the god of cheer or the belly," is one of the characters, a circumstance which an imaginative boy of ten, named John Milton, was not to forget. "Pan's Anniversary," late in the reign of James, proclaimed that Jonson had not yet forgotten how to write exquisite lyrics, and "The Gipsies Metamorphosed" displayed the old drollery and broad humorous stroke still unimpaired and unmatchable. These, too, and the earlier years of Charles were the days of the Apollo Room of the Devil Tavern where Jonson presided, the absolute monarch of English literary Bohemia. We hear of a room blazoned about with Jonson's own judicious 'Leges Convivales' in letters of gold, of a company made up of the choicest spirits of the time, devotedly attached to their veteran dictator, his reminiscences, opinions, affections, and enmities. And we hear, too, of valorous potations; but in the words of Herrick addressed to his master, Jonson, at the Devil Tavern, as at the Dog, the Triple Tun, and at the Mermaid, "We such clusters had As made us nobly wild, not mad, And yet each verse of thine Outdid the meat, outdid the frolic wine."

But the patronage of the court failed in the days of King Charles, though Jonson was not without royal favours; and the old poet returned to the stage, producing, between 1625 and 1633, "The Staple of News," "The New Inn," "The Magnetic Lady," and "The Tale of a Tub," the last doubtless revised from a much earlier comedy. None of these plays met with any marked success, although the scathing generalisation of Dryden that designated them "Jonson's dotages" is unfair to their genuine merits. Thus the idea of an office for the gathering, proper dressing, and promulgation of news (wild flight of the fancy in its time) was an excellent subject for satire on the existing absurdities among the newsmongers; although as much can hardly be said for "The Magnetic Lady," who, in her bounty, draws to her personages of differing humours to reconcile them in the end according to the alternative title, or "Humours Reconciled."

These last plays of the old dramatist revert to caricature and the hard lines of allegory; the moralist is more than ever present, the satire degenerates into personal lampoon, especially of his sometime friend, Inigo Jones, who appears unworthily to have used his influence at court against the broken-down old poet. And now disease claimed Jonson, and he was bedridden for months. He had succeeded Middleton in 1628 as Chronologer to the City of London, but lost the post for not fulfilling its duties. King Charles befriended him, and even commissioned him to write still for the entertainment of the court; and he was not without the sustaining hand of noble patrons and devoted friends among the younger poets who were proud to be "sealed of the tribe of Ben."

Jonson died, August 6, 1637, and a second folio of his works, which he had been some time gathering, was printed in 1640, bearing in its various parts dates ranging from 1630 to 1642. It included all the plays mentioned in the foregoing paragraphs, excepting "The Case is Altered;" the masques, some fifteen, that date between 1617 and 1630; another collection of lyrics and occasional poetry called "Underwoods, including some further entertainments; a translation of "Horace's Art of Poetry" (also published in a vicesimo quarto in 1640), and certain fragments and ingatherings which the poet would hardly have included himself. These last comprise the fragment (less than seventy lines) of a tragedy called "Mortimer his Fall," and three acts of a pastoral drama of much beauty and poetic spirit, "The Sad Shepherd." There is also the exceedingly interesting 'English Grammar' "made by Ben Jonson for the benefit of all strangers out of his observation of the English language now spoken and in use," in Latin and English; and 'Timber, or discoveries' "made upon men and matter as they have flowed out of his daily reading, or had their reflux to his peculiar notion of the times." The 'Discoveries', as it is usually called, is a commonplace book such as many literary men have kept, in which their reading was chronicled, passages that took their fancy translated or transcribed, and their passing opinions noted. Many passage of Jonson's 'Discoveries' are literal translations from the authors he chanced to be reading, with the reference, noted or not, as the accident of the moment prescribed. At times he follows the line of Macchiavelli's argument as to the nature and conduct of princes; at others he clarifies his own conception of poetry and poets by recourse to Aristotle. He finds a choice paragraph on eloquence in Seneca the elder and applies it to his own recollection of Bacon's power as an orator; and another on facile and ready genius, and translates it, adapting it to his recollection of his fellow-playwright, Shakespeare. To call such passages—which Jonson never intended for publication—plagiarism, is to obscure the significance of words. To disparage his memory by citing them is a preposterous use of scholarship. Jonson's prose, both in his dramas, in the descriptive comments of his masques, and in the 'Discoveries', is characterised by clarity and vigorous directness, nor is it wanting in a fine sense of form or in the subtler graces of diction.

When Jonson died there was a project for a handsome monument to his memory. But the Civil War was at hand, and the project failed. A memorial, not insufficient, was carved on the stone covering his grave in one of the aisles of Westminster Abbey: "O rare Ben Jonson."

FELIX E. SCHELLING.
THE COLLEGE,
PHILADELPHIA, U.S.A.

THE INNS OF COURT

I UNDERSTAND you, Gentlemen, not your houses: and a worthy succession of you, to all time, as being born the judges of these studies. When I wrote this poem, I had friendship with divers in your societies; who, as they were great names in learning, so they were no less examples of living. Of them, and then, that I say no more, it was not despised. Now that the printer, by a doubled charge, thinks it worthy a longer life than commonly the air of such things doth promise, I am careful to put it a servant to their pleasures, who are the inheritors of the first favour born it. Yet, I command it lie not in the way of your more noble and useful studies to the public: for so I shall suffer for it. But when the gown and cap is off, and the lord of liberty reigns, then, to take it in your hands, perhaps may make some bencher, tincted with humanity, read and not repent him.

By your true honourer,
BEN JONSON.

DRAMATIS PERSONAE

ASPER, the Presenter.
MACILENTE.
PUNTARVOLO,—his Lady.—Waiting Gent.—Huntsman.—
Servingmen.—Dog and Cat.
CARLO BUFFONE.
FASTIDIOUS BRISK,—Cinedo, his Page.
DELIRO, FALLACE,—Fido, their Servant.—Musicians.
SAVIOLINA.
SORDIDO.—His Hind.
FUNGOSO.—Tailor, Haberdasher, Shoemaker
SOGLIARDO.
SHIFT.—Rustics.
NOTARY.
CLOVE, ORANGE.—A Groom.—Drawers.—Constable, and
Officers.
GREX.—CORDATUS—MITIS.

THE CHARACTERS OF THE PERSONS

ASPER, he is of an ingenious and free spirit, eager and constant in
reproof, without fear controlling the world's abuses. One whom no
servile hope of gain, or frosty apprehension of danger, can make
to be a parasite, either to time, place, or opinion.
MACILENTE, a man well parted, a sufficient scholar, and travelled;
who, wanting that place in the world's account which he thinks

his merit capable of, falls into such an envious apoplexy, with which his judgment is so dazzled and distasted, that he grows violently impatient of any opposite happiness in another.

PUNTARVOLO, a vain-glorious knight, over-englishing his travels, and wholly consecrated to singularity; the very Jacob's staff of compliment; a sir that hath lived to see the revolution of time in most of his apparel. Of presence good enough, but so palpably affected to his own praise, that for want of flatterers he commends himself, to the floutage of his own family. He deals upon returns, and strange performances, resolving, in despite of public derision, to stick to his own fashion, phrase, and gesture.

CARLO BUFFONE, a public, scurrilous, and profane jester, that more swift than Circe, with absurd similes, will transform any person into deformity. A good feast-hound or banquet-beagle, that will scent you out a supper some three miles off, and swear to his patrons, damn him! he came in oars, when he was but wafted over in a sculler. A slave that hath an extraordinary gift in pleasing his palate, and will swill up more sack at a sitting than would make all the guard a posset. His religion is railing, and his discourse ribaldry.

FASTIDIOUS BRISK, a neat, spruce, affecting courtier, one that wears clothes well, and in fashion; practiseth by his glass how to salute; speaks good remnants, notwithstanding the base viol and tobacco; swears tersely and with variety; cares not what lady's favour he belies, or great man's familiarity: a good property to perfume the boot of a coach. He will borrow another man's horse to praise, and backs him as his own. Or, for a need, on foot can post himself into credit with his merchant, only with the gingle of his spur, and the jerk of his wand.

DELIRO, a good doting citizen, who, it is thought, might be of the common-council for his wealth; a fellow sincerely besotted on his own wife, and so wrapt with a conceit of her perfections, that he simply holds himself unworthy of her. And, in that hood-wink'd humour,

36

lives more like a suitor than a husband; standing in as true dread of her displeasure, as when he first made love to her. He doth sacrifice two-pence in juniper to her every morning before she rises, and wakes her with villainous-out-of-tune music, which she out of her contempt (though not out of her judgment) is sure to dislike.

FALLACE, Deliro's wife, and idol; a proud mincing peat, and as perverse as he is officious. She dotes as perfectly upon the courtier, as her husband doth on her, and only wants the face to be dishonest.

SAVIOLINA, a court-lady, whose weightiest praise is a light wit, admired by herself, and one more, her servant Brisk.

SORDIDO, a wretched hob-nailed chuff, whose recreation is reading of almanacks; and felicity, foul weather. One that never pray'd but for a lean dearth, and ever wept in a fat harvest.

FUNGOSO, the son of Sordido, and a student; one that has revelled in his time, and follows the fashion afar off, like a spy. He makes it the whole bent of his endeavours to wring sufficient means from his wretched father, to put him in the courtiers' cut; at which he earnestly aims, but so unluckily, that he still lights short a suit.

SOGLIARDO, an essential clown, brother to Sordido, yet so enamoured of the name of a gentleman, that he will have it, though he buys it. He comes up every term to learn to take tobacco, and see new motions. He is in his kingdom when in company where he may be well laughed at.

SHIFT, a thread-bare shark; one that never was a soldier, yet lives upon lendings. His profession is skeldring and odling, his bank Paul's, and his warehouse Picthatch. Takes up single testons upon oaths, till doomsday. Falls under executions of three shillings, and enters into five-groat bonds. He way-lays the reports of services, and cons them without book, damning himself he came new from them, when all the while he was taking the diet in the bawdyhouse, or lay pawned in his chamber for rent and victuals. He is of that admirable and happy memory, that he will salute one for an old acquaintance that he never saw in his life before. He usurps upon cheats, quarrels, and robberies, which he never did, only to get him a name. His chief exercises are, taking the whiff, squiring a cockatrice, and making privy searches for imparters.

CLOVE and ORANGE, an inseparable case of coxcombs, city born; the Gemini, or twins of foppery; that like a pair of wooden foils, are fit for nothing but to be practised upon. Being well flattered they'll lend money, and repent when they have done. Their glory is to invite players, and make suppers. And in company of better rank, to avoid the suspect of insufficiency, will inforce their ignorance most desperately, to set upon the understanding of any thing. Orange is the most humorous of the two, (whose small portion of juice being squeezed out,) Clove serves to stick him with commendations.

CORDATUS, the author's friend; a man inly acquainted with the scope and drift of his plot; of a discreet and understanding judgment; and has the place of a moderator.

MITIS, is a person of no action, and therefore we afford him no character.

THE STAGE. After the second sounding.

ENTER CORDATUS, ASPER, AND MITIS.

COR. Nay, my dear Asper.
MIT. Stay your mind.
ASP. Away!
    Who is so patient of this impious world,
    That he can check his spirit, or rein his tongue?

Or who hath such a dead unfeeling sense,
That heaven's horrid thunders cannot wake?
To see the earth crack'd with the weight of sin,
Hell gaping under us, and o'er our heads
Black, ravenous ruin, with her sail-stretch'd wings,
Ready to sink us down, and cover us.
Who can behold such prodigies as these,
And have his lips seal'd up? Not I: my soul
Was never ground into such oily colours,
To flatter vice, and daub iniquity:
But, with an armed and resolved hand,
I'll strip the ragged follies of the time
Naked as at their birth—

COR. Be not too bold.
ASP. You trouble me—and with a whip of steel,
Print wounding lashes in their iron ribs.
I fear no mood stamp'd in a private brow,
When I am pleased t'unmask a public vice.
I fear no strumpet's drugs, nor ruffian's stab,
Should I detect their hateful luxuries:
No broker's usurer's, or lawyer's gripe,
Were I disposed to say, they are all corrupt.
I fear no courtier's frown, should I applaud
The easy flexure of his supple hams.
Tut, these are so innate and popular,
That drunken custom would not shame to laugh,
In scorn, at him, that should but dare to tax 'em:
And yet, not one of these, but knows his works,
Knows what damnation is, the devil, and hell;
Yet hourly they persist, grow rank in sin,
Puffing their souls away in perjurous air,
To cherish their extortion, pride, or lusts.

MIT. Forbear, good Asper; be not like your name.

ASP. O, but to such whose faces are all zeal,
    And, with the words of Hercules, invade
    Such crimes as these! that will not smell of sin,
    But seem as they were made of sanctity!
    Religion in their garments, and their hair
    Cut shorter than their eye-brows! when the conscience
    Is vaster than the ocean, and devours
    More wretches than the counters.
MIT. Gentle Asper,
    Contain our spirits in more stricter bounds,
    And be not thus transported with the violence
    Of your strong thoughts.
COX. Unless your breath had power,
    To melt the world, and mould it new again,
    It is in vain to spend it in these moods.
ASP. [TURNING TO THE STAGE.]
    I not observed this thronged round till now !
    Gracious and kind spectators, you are welcome;
    Apollo and Muses feast your eyes
    With graceful objects, and may our Minerva
    Answer your hopes, unto their largest strain!
    Yet here mistake me not, judicious friends;
    I do not this, to beg your patience,
    Or servilely to fawn on your applause,
    Like some dry brain, despairing in his merit.
    Let me be censured by the austerest brow,
    Where I want art or judgment, tax me freely.
    Let envious censors, with their broadest eyes,
    Look through and through me, I pursue no favour;
    Only vouchsafe me your attentions,
    And I will give you music worth your ears.
    O, how I hate the monstrousness of time,

Where every servile imitating spirit,
Plagued with an itching leprosy of wit,
In a mere halting fury, strives to fling
His ulcerous body in the Thespian spring,
And straight leaps forth a poet! but as lame
As Vulcan, or the founder of Cripplegate.

MIT. In faith this humour will come ill to some,
    You will be thought to be too peremptory.

ASP. This humour? good! and why this humour, Mitis?
    Nay, do not turn, but answer.

MIT. Answer, what?

ASP. I will not stir your patience, pardon me,
    I urged it for some reasons, and the rather
    To give these ignorant well-spoken days
    Some taste of their abuse of this word humour.

COR. O, do not let your purpose fall, good Asper;
    It cannot but arrive most acceptable,
    Chiefly to such as have the happiness
    Daily to see how the poor innocent word
    Is rack'd and tortured.

MIT. Ay, I pray you proceed.

ASP. Ha, what? what is't?

COR. For the abuse of humour.

ASP. O, I crave pardon, I had lost my thoughts.
    Why humour, as 'tis 'ens', we thus define it,
    To be a quality of air, or water,
    And in itself holds these two properties,
    Moisture and fluxure: as, for demonstration,
    Pour water on this floor, 'twill wet and run:
    Likewise the air, forced through a horn or trumpet,
    Flows instantly away, and leaves behind
    A kind of dew; and hence we do conclude,

That whatsoe'er hath fluxure and humidity,
As wanting power to contain itself,
Is humour. So in every human body,
The choler, melancholy, phlegm, and blood,
By reason that they flow continually
In some one part, and are not continent,
Receive the name of humours. Now thus far
It may, by metaphor, apply itself
Unto the general disposition:
As when some one peculiar quality
Doth so possess a man, that it doth draw
All his affects, his spirits, and his powers,
In their confluctions, all to run one way,
This may be truly said to be a humour
But that a rook, by wearing a pyed feather,
The cable hat-band, or the three-piled ruff,
A yard of shoe-tye, or the Switzer's knot
On his French garters, should affect a humour!
O, it is more than most ridiculous.
COR. He speaks pure truth; now if an idiot
Have but an apish or fantastic strain,
It is his humour.
ASP. Well, I will scourge those apes,
And to these courteous eyes oppose a mirror,
As large as is the stage whereon we act;
Where they shall see the time's deformity
Anatomised in every nerve, and sinew,
With constant courage, and contempt of fear.
MIT. Asper, (I urge it as your friend,) take heed,
The days are dangerous, full of exception,
And men are grown impatient of reproof.
ASP. Ha, ha!

You might as well have told me, yond' is heaven,
This earth, these men, and all had moved alike.—
Do not I know the time's condition?
Yes, Mitis, and their souls; and who they be
That either will or can except against me.
None but a sort of fools, so sick in taste,
That they contemn all physic of the mind,
And like gall'd camels, kick at every touch.
Good men, and virtuous spirits, that loath their vices,
Will cherish my free labours, love my lines,
And with the fervour of their shining grace
Make my brain fruitful, to bring forth more objects,
Worthy their serious and intentive eyes.
But why enforce I this? as fainting? no.
If any here chance to behold himself,
Let him not dare to challenge me of wrong;
For, if he shame to have his follies known,
First he should shame to act 'em: my strict hand
Was made to seize on vice, and with a gripe
Squeeze out the humour of such spongy souls,
As lick up every idle vanity.
COR. Why, this is right furor poeticus!
Kind gentlemen, we hope your patience
Will yet conceive the best, or entertain
This supposition, that a madman speaks.
ASP. What, are you ready there? Mitis, sit down,
And my Cordatus. Sound ho! and begin.
I leave you two, as censors, to sit here:
Observe what I present, and liberally
Speak your opinions upon every scene,
As it shall pass the view of these spectators.
Nay, now y'are tedious, sirs; for shame begin.

43

And, Mitis, note me; if in all this front
You can espy a gallant of this mark,
Who, to be thought one of the judicious,
Sits with his arms thus wreath'd, his hat pull'd here,
Cries mew, and nods, then shakes his empty head,
Will shew more several motions in his face
Than the new London, Rome, or Niniveh,
And, now and then, breaks a dry biscuit jest,
Which, that it may more easily be chew'd,
He steeps in his own laughter.

COR. Why, will that
Make it be sooner swallowed?

ASP. O, assure you.
Or if it did not, yet as Horace sings,
Mean cates are welcome still to hungry guests.

COR. 'Tis true; but why should we observe them, Asper?

ASP. O, I would know 'em; for in such assemblies
They are more infectious than the pestilence:
And therefore I would give them pills to purge,
And make them fit for fair societies.
How monstrous and detested is't to see
A fellow that has neither art nor brain,
Sit like an Aristarchus, or start ass,
Taking men's lines with a tobacco face,
In snuff still spitting, using his wry'd looks,
In nature of a vice, to wrest and turn
The good aspect of those that shall sit near him,
From what they do behold! O, 'tis most vile.

MIT. Nay, Asper.

ASP. Peace, Mitis, I do know your thought;
You'll say, your guests here will except at this:
Pish! you are too timorous, and full of doubt.
Then he, a patient, shall reject all physic,

'Cause the physician tells him, you are sick:
Or, if I say, that he is vicious,
You will not hear of virtue. Come, you are fond.
Shall I be so extravagant, to think,
That happy judgments, and composed spirits,
Will challenge me for taxing such as these?
I am ashamed.
COR. Nay, but good, pardon us;
We must not bear this peremptory sail,
But use our best endeavours how to please.
ASP. Why, therein I commend your careful thoughts,
And I will mix with you in industry
To please: but whom? attentive auditors,
Such as will join their profit with their pleasure,
And come to feed their understanding parts:
For these I'll prodigally spread myself,
And speak away my spirit into air;
For these, I'll melt my brain into invention,
Coin new conceits, and hang my richest words
As polish'd jewels in their bounteous ears?
But stay, I lose myself, and wrong their patience:
If I dwell here, they'll not begin, I see.
Friends, sit you still, and entertain this troop
With some familiar and by-conference,
I'll hast them sound. Now, gentlemen, I go
To turn an actor, and a humorist,
Where, ere I do resume my present person,
We hope to make the circles of your eyes
Flow with distilled laughter: if we fail,
We must impute it to this only chance,
Art hath an enemy call'd ignorance.

[EXIT.

COR. How do you like his spirit, Mitis?

MIT. I should like it much better, if he were less confident.

COR. Why, do you suspect his merit?

MIT. No; but I fear this will procure him much envy.

COR. O, that sets the stronger seal on his desert: if he had no enemies, I should esteem his fortunes most wretched at this instant.

MIT. You have seen his play, Cordatus: pray you, how is it?

COR. Faith, sir, I must refrain to judge; only this I can say of it, 'tis strange, and of a particular kind by itself, somewhat like 'Vetus Comoedia'; a work that hath bounteously pleased me; how it will answer the general expectation, I know not.

MIT. Does he observe all the laws of comedy in it?

COR. What laws mean you?

MIT. Why, the equal division of it into acts and scenes, according to the Terentian manner; his true number of actors; the furnishing of the scene with Grex or Chorus, and that the whole argument fall within compass of a day's business.

COR. O no, these are too nice observations.

MIT. They are such as must be received, by your favour, or it cannot be authentic.

COR. Troth, I can discern no such necessity.

MIT. No!

COR. No, I assure you, signior. If those laws you speak of had been delivered us 'ab initio', and in their present virtue and perfection, there had been some reason of obeying their powers; but 'tis extant, that that which we call 'Comoedia', was at first nothing but a simple and continued song, sung by one only person, till Susario invented a second; after him, Epicharmus a third; Phormus and Chionides devised to have four actors, with a prologue and chorus; to which Cratinus, long after, added a fifth and sixth: Eupolis, more; Aristophanes, more than they; every man in the dignity of his spirit and judgment supplied something. And, though that in him this kind of poem appeared absolute, and fully perfect, yet how is the face of it changed since, in Menander, Philemon, Cecilius, Plautus, and the rest! who have utterly excluded the chorus, altered the property of the persons, their names, and natures, and augmented it with all liberty, according to the elegancy and disposition of those times wherein they wrote. I see not then, but we should enjoy the same license, or free power to illustrate and heighten our invention, as they did; and not be tied to those strict and regular forms which the niceness of a few, who are nothing but form, would thrust upon us.

MIT. Well, we will not dispute of this now; but what's his scene?

COR. Marry, 'Insula Fortunata', sir.

MIT. O, the Fortunate Island: mass, he has bound himself to a strict law there.

COR. Why so?

MIT. He cannot lightly alter the scene, without crossing the seas.

COR. He needs not, having a whole island to run through, I think.

MIT. No! how comes it then, that in some one play we see so many seas, countries, and kingdoms, passed over with such admirable dexterity?

COR. O, that but shews how well the authors can travel in their vocation, and outrun the apprehension of their auditory. But, leaving this, I would they would begin at once: this protraction is able to sour the best-settled patience in the theatre. [THE THIRD SOUNDING.

MIT. They have answered your wish, sir; they sound.

COR. O, here comes the Prologue. [ENTER PROLOGUE. Now, sir, if you had staid a little longer, I meant to have spoke your prologue for you i'faith.

PROL. Marry, with all my heart, sir, you shall do it yet, and I thank you. [GOING.

COR. Nay, nay, stay, stay; hear you?

PROL. You could not have studied to have done me a greater benefit at the instant; for I protest to you, I am unperfect, and, had I spoke it, I must of necessity have been out.

COR. Why, but do you speak this seriously?

PROL. Seriously! ay, wit's my help, do I; and esteem myself indebted to your kindness for it.

COR. For what?

PROL. Why, for undertaking the prologue for me.

COR. How! did I undertake it for you?

PROL. Did you! I appeal to all these gentlemen, whether you did or no. Come, come, it pleases you to cast a strange look on't now; but 'twill not serve.

COR. 'Fore me, but it must serve; and therefore speak your prologue.

PROL. An I do, let me die poisoned with some venomous hiss, and never live to look as high as the two-penny room again.

[EXIT.

MIT. He has put you to it, sir.

COR. 'Sdeath, what a humorous fellow is this! Gentlemen, good faith I can speak no prologue, howsoever his weak wit has had the fortune to make this strong use of me here before you: but I protest—

[ENTER CARLO BUFFONE, FOLLOWED BY A BOY WITH WINE. CAR. Come, come, leave these fustian protestations; away, come, I cannot abide these grey-headed ceremonies. Boy, fetch me a glass quickly, I may bid these gentlemen welcome; give them a health here.

[EXIT BOY.] I mar'le whose wit it was to put a prologue in yond' sackbut's mouth; they might well think he'd be out of tune, and yet you'd play upon him too.

COR. Hang him, dull block!

CAR. O, good words, good words; a well-timber'd fellow, he would have made a good column, an he had been thought on, when the house was a building—[RE-ENTER BOY WITH GLASSES.. O, art thou

48

come? Well said; give me, boy; fill so! Here's a cup of wine sparkles like a diamond. Gentlewomen (I am sworn to put them in first) and gentlemen, around, in place of a bad prologue, I drink this good draught to your health here, Canary, the very elixir and spirit of wine. [DRINKS.] This is that our poet calls Castalian liquor, when he comes abroad now and then, once in a fortnight, and makes a good meal among players, where he has 'caninum appetitum'; marry, at home he keeps a good philosophical diet, beans and butter-milk; an honest pure rogue, he will take you off three, four, five of these, one after another, and look villainously when he has done, like a one-headed Cerberus.—He does not hear me, I hope.—And then, when his belly is well ballaced, and his brain rigged a little, he snails away withal, as though he would work wonders when he comes home. He has made a play here, and he calls it, 'Every Man out of his Humour': but an he get me out of the humour he has put me in, I'll trust none of his tribe again while I live. Gentles, all I can say for him is, you are welcome. I could wish my bottle here amongst you; but there's an old rule, No pledging your own health. Marry, if any here be thirsty for it, their best way (that I know) is, sit still, seal up their lips, and drink so much of the play in at their ears.

[EXIT.

MIT. What may this fellow be, Cordatus?

COR. Faith, if the time will suffer his description, I'll give it you. He is one, the author calls him Carlo Buffone, an impudent common jester, a violent railer, and an incomprehensible epicure; one whose company is desired of all men, but beloved of none; he will sooner lose his soul than a jest, and profane even the most holy things, to excite laughter: no honourable or reverend personage whatsoever can come within the reach of his eye, but is turned into all manner of variety, by his adulterate similes.

MIT. You paint forth a monster.

COR. He will prefer all countries before his native, and thinks he can never sufficiently, or with admiration enough, deliver his affectionate conceit of foreign atheistical policies. But stay—[ENTER MACILENTE. Observe these: he'll appear himself anon.

MIT. O, this is your envious man, Macilente, I think.

COR. The same, sir.

ACT I

SCENE I.—The Country.

ENTER MACILENTE, WITH A BOOK.

MACI. "Viri est, fortunae caecitatem facile ferre."
 'Tis true; but, Stoic, where, in the vast world,
 Doth that man breathe, that can so much command
 His blood and his affection? Well, I see
 I strive in vain to cure my wounded soul;
 For every cordial that my thoughts apply
 Turns to a corsive and doth eat it farther.
 There is no taste in this philosophy;
 'Tis like a potion that a man should drink,
 But turns his stomach with the sight of it.
 I am no such pill'd Cynick to believe,
 That beggary is the only happiness;
 Or with a number of these patient fools,
 To sing: "My mind to me a kingdom is,"
 When the lank hungry belly barks for food,
 I look into the world, and there I meet
 With objects, that do strike my blood-shot eyes
 Into my brain: where, when I view myself,

Having before observ'd this man is great,
Mighty and fear'd; that lov'd and highly favour'd:
A third thought wise and learn'd; a fourth rich,
And therefore honour'd; a fifth rarely featur'd;
A sixth admired for his nuptial fortunes:
When I see these, I say, and view myself,
I wish the organs of my sight were crack'd;
And that the engine of my grief could cast
Mine eyeballs, like two globes of wildfire, forth,
To melt this unproportion'd frame of nature.
Oh, they are thoughts that have transfix'd my heart,
And often, in the strength of apprehension,
Made my cold passion stand upon my face,
Like drops of dew on a stiff cake of ice.

COR. This alludes well to that of the poet,
    "Invidus suspirat, gemit, incutitque dentes,
    Sudat frigidus, intuens quod odit."

MIT. O, peace, you break the scene.
    [ENTER SOGLIARDO AND CARLO BUFFONE.

MACI. Soft, who be these?
    I'll lay me down awhile till they be past.
    [LIES DOWN.

CAR. Signior, note this gallant, I pray you.

MIT. What is he?

CAR. A tame rook, you'll take him presently; list.

SOG. Nay, look you, Carlo; this is my humour now! I have land and
    money, my friends left me well, and I will be a gentleman whatsoever
    it cost me.

CAR. A most gentlemanlike resolution.

SOG. Tut! an I take an humour of a thing once, I am like your tailor's
    needle, I go through: but, for my name, signior, how think you? will

it not serve for a gentleman's name, when the signior is put to it, ha?

CAR. Let me hear; how is it?

SOG. Signior Insulso Sogliardo: methinks it sounds well.

CAR. O excellent! tut! an all fitted to your name, you might very well stand for a gentleman: I know many Sogliardos gentlemen.

SOG. Why, and for my wealth I might be a justice of peace.

CAR. Ay, and a constable for your wit.

SOG. All this is my lordship you see here, and those farms you came by.

CAR. Good steps to gentility too, marry: but, Sogliardo, if you affect to be a gentleman indeed, you must observe all the rare qualities, humours, and compliments of a gentleman.

SOG. I know it, signior, and if you please to instruct, I am not too good to learn, I'll assure you.

CAR. Enough, sir.—I'll make admirable use in the projection of my medicine upon this lump of copper here. [ASIDE]—I'll bethink me for you, sir.

SOG. Signior, I will both pay you, and pray you, and thank you, and think on you.

COR. Is this not purely good?

MACI. S'blood, why should such a prick-ear'd hind as this Be rich, ha? a fool! such a transparent gull That may be seen through! wherefore should he have land, Houses, and lordships? O, I could eat my entrails, And sink my soul into the earth with sorrow.

CAR. First, to be an accomplished gentleman, that is, a gentleman of the time, you must give over housekeeping in the country, and live altogether in the city amongst gallants: where, at your first appearance, 'twere good you turn'd four or five hundred acres of your best land into two or three trunks of apparel—you may do it without going to a conjurer—and be sure you mix yourself still with such as flourish in the spring of the fashion, and are least popular; study their carriage and behaviour in all; learn to play at primero and passage, and ever (when you lose) have two or three peculiar oaths to swear by, that no man else swears: but, above all, protest in your play, and affirm, "Upon your credit, As you are a true gentleman", at every cast; you may do it with a safe conscience, I warrant you.

SOG. O admirable rare! he cannot choose but be a gentleman that has these excellent gifts: more, more, I beseech you.

CAR. You must endeavour to feed cleanly at your ordinary, sit melancholy, and pick your teeth when you cannot speak: and when you come to plays, be humorous, look with a good starch'd face, and ruffle your brow like a new boot, laugh at nothing but your own jests, or else as the noblemen laugh. That's a special grace you must observe.

SAG. I warrant you, sir.

CAR. Ay, and sit on the stage and flout, provided you have a good suit.

SOG. O, I'll have a suit only for that, sir.

CAR. You must talk much of your kindred and allies.

SOG. Lies! no, signior, I shall not need to do so, I have kindred in the city to talk of: I have a niece is a merchant's wife; and a nephew, my brother Sordido's son, of the Inns of court.

CAR. O, but you must pretend alliance with courtiers and great persons: and ever when you are to dine or sup in any strange presence, hire a fellow with a great chain, (though it be copper, it's no matter,) to bring you letters, feign'd from such a nobleman, or such a knight, or such a lady, "To their worshipful, right rare, and nobly qualified friend and kinsman, signior Insulso Sogliardo": give yourself style enough. And there, while you intend circumstances of news, or enquiry of their health, or so, one of your familiars whom you must carry about you still, breaks it up, as 'twere in a jest, and reads it publicly at the table: at which you must seem to take as unpardonable offence, as if he had torn your mistress's colours, or breath'd upon her picture, and pursue it with that hot grace, as if you would advance a challenge upon it presently.

SOG. Stay, I do not like that humour of challenge, it may be accepted; but I'll tell you what's my humour now, I will do this: I will take occasion of sending one of my suits to the tailor's, to have the pocket repaired, or so; and there such a letter as you talk of, broke open and all shall be left; O, the tailor will presently give out what I am, upon the reading of it, worth twenty of your gallants.

CAR. But then you must put on an extreme face of discontentment at your man's negligence.

SOG. O, so I will, and beat him too: I'll have a man for the purpose.

MAC. You may; you have land and crowns: O partial fate!

CAR. Mass, well remember'd, you must keep your men gallant at the first, fine pied liveries laid with good gold lace; there's no loss in it, they may rip it off and pawn it when they lack victuals.

SOG. By 'r Lady, that is chargeable, signior, 'twill bring a man in debt.

CAR. Debt! why that's the more for your credit, sir: it's an excellent policy to owe much in these days, if you note it.

SOG. As how, good signior? I would fain be a politician.

CAR. O! look where you are indebted any great sum, your creditor observes you with no less regard, than if he were bound to you for some huge benefit, and will quake to give you the least cause of offence, lest he lose his money. I assure you, in these times, no man has his servant more obsequious and pliant, than gentlemen their creditors: to whom, if at any time you pay but a moiety, or a fourth part, it comes more acceptably than if you gave them a new-year's gift.

SOG. I perceive you, sir: I will take up, and bring myself in credit, sure.

CAR. Marry this, always beware you commerce not with bankrupts, or poor needy Ludgathians; they are impudent creatures, turbulent spirits, they care not what violent tragedies they stir, nor how they play fast and loose with a poor gentleman's fortunes, to get their own. Marry, these rich fellows that have the world, or the better part of it, sleeping in their counting-houses, they are ten times more placable, they; either fear, hope, or modesty, restrains them from offering any outrages: but this is nothing to your followers, you shall not run a penny more in arrearage for them, an you list, yourself.

SOG. No! how should I keep 'em then?

CAR. Keep 'em! 'sblood, let them keep themselves, they are no sheep, are they? what, you shall come in houses, where plate, apparel, jewels, and divers other pretty commodities lie negligently scattered, and I would have those Mercuries follow me, I trow, should remember they had not their fingers for nothing.

SOG. That's not so good, methinks.

CAR. Why, after you have kept them a fortnight, or so, and shew'd them enough to the world, you may turn them away, and keep no more but a boy, it's enough.

SOG. Nay, my humour is not for boys, I'll keep men, an I keep any; and I'll give coats, that's my humour: but I lack a cullisen.

CAR. Why, now you ride to the city, you may buy one; I'll bring you where you shall have your choice for money.

SOG. Can you, sir?

CAR. O, ay: you shall have one take measure of you, and make you a coat of arms to fit you, of what fashion you will.

SOG. By word of mouth, I thank you, signior; I'll be once a little prodigal in a humour, i'faith, and have a most prodigious coat.

MAC. Torment and death! break head and brain at once, To be deliver'd of your fighting issue. Who can endure to see blind Fortune dote thus? To be enamour'd on this dusty turf, This clod, a whoreson puck-fist! O G—! I could run wild with grief now, to behold The rankness of her bounties, that doth breed Such bulrushes; these mushroom gentlemen, That shoot up in a night to place and worship.

CAR. [SEEING MACILENTE.] Let him alone; some stray, some stray.

SOG. Nay, I will examine him before I go, sure.

CAR. The lord of the soil has all wefts and strays here, has he not?

SOG. Yes, sir.

CAR. Faith then I pity the poor fellow, he's fallen into a fool's hands. [ASIDE.

SOG. Sirrah, who gave you a commission to lie in my lordship?

MAC. Your lordship!

SOG. How! my lordship? do you know me, sir?

MAC. I do know you, sir.

CAR. He answers him like an echo. [ASIDE.

SOG. Why, Who am I, sir?

MAC. One of those that fortune favours.

CAR. The periphrasis of a fool. I'll observe this better. [ASIDE.

SOG. That fortune favours! how mean you that, friend?

MAC. I mean simply: that you are one that lives not by your wits.

SOG. By my wits! no sir, I scorn to live by my wits, I. I have better means, I tell thee, than to take such base courses, as to live by my wits. What, dost thou think I live by my wits?

MAC. Methinks, jester, you should not relish this well.

CAR. Ha! does he know me?

MAC. Though yours be the worst use a man can put his wit to, of thousands, to prostitute it at every tavern and ordinary; yet, methinks, you should have turn'd your broadside at this, and have been ready with an apology, able to sink this hulk of ignorance into the bottom and depth of his contempt.

CAR. Oh, 'tis Macilente! Signior, you are well encountered; how is it? O, we must not regard what he says, man, a trout, a shallow fool, he has no more brain than a butterfly, a mere stuft suit; he looks like a musty bottle new wicker'd, his head's the cork, light, light! [ASIDE TO MACILENTE.]—I am glad to see you so well return'd, signior.

MAC. You are! gramercy, good Janus.

SOG. Is he one of your acquaintance? I love him the better for that.

CAR. Od's precious, come away, man, what do you mean? an you knew him as I do, you'd shun him as you would do the plague.

SOG. Why, sir?

CAR. O, he's a black fellow, take heed of him.

SOG. Is he a scholar, or a soldier?

CAR. Both, both; a lean mongrel, he looks as if he were chop-fallen, with barking at other men's good fortunes: 'ware how you offend him; he carries oil and fire in his pen, will scald where it drops: his spirit is like powder, quick, violent; he'll blow a man up with a jest: I fear him worse than a rotten wall does the cannon; shake an hour after at the report. Away, come not near him.

SOG. For God's sake let's be gone; an he be a scholar, you know I cannot abide him; I had as lieve see a cockatrice, specially as cockatrices go now.

CAR. What, you'll stay, signior? this gentleman Sogliardo, and I, are to visit the knight Puntarvolo, and from thence to the city; we shall meet there.

[EXIT WITH SOGLIARDO.

MAC. Ay, when I cannot shun you, we will meet.
    'Tis strange! of all the creatures I have seen,
    I envy not this Buffone, for indeed
    Neither his fortunes nor his parts deserve it:
    But I do hate him, as I hate the devil,
    Or that brass-visaged monster Barbarism.
    O, 'tis an open-throated, black-mouth'd cur,
    That bites at all, but eats on those that feed him.
    A slave, that to your face will, serpent-like,
    Creep on the ground, as he would eat the dust,
    And to your back will turn the tail, and sting
    More deadly than the scorpion: stay, who's this?
    Now, for my soul, another minion
    Of the old lady Chance's! I'll observe him.

[ENTER SORDIDO WITH AN ALMANACK IN HIS HAND.

SORD. O rare! good, good, good, good, good!
    I thank my stars, I thank my stars for it.

MAC. Said I not true? doth not his passion speak
    Out of my divination? O my senses,
    Why lost you not your powers, and become
    Dull'd, if not deaded, with this spectacle?
    I know him, it is Sordido, the farmer,
    A boor, and brother to that swine was here.
    [ASIDE.
SORD. Excellent, excellent, excellent! as I would wish, as I would wish.
MAC. See how the strumpet fortune tickles him,
    And makes him swoon with laughter, O, O, O!
SORD. Ha, ha, ha! I will not sow my grounds this year. Let me see, what
    harvest shall we have? "June, July?"
MAC. What, is't a prognostication raps him so?
SORD. "The 20, 21, 22 days, rain and wind." O good, good! "the 23, and
    24, rain and some wind," good! "the 25, rain," good still! "26, 27,
    28, wind and some rain"; would it had been rain and some wind!
    well, 'tis good, when it can be no better. "29, inclining to rain":
    inclining to rain! that's not so good now: "30, and 31, wind and no
    rain": no rain! 'slid, stay: this is worse and worse: What says he of St.
    Swithin's? turn back, look, "saint Swithin's: no rain!"
MAC. O, here's a precious, dirty, damned rogue,
    That fats himself with expectation
    Of rotten weather, and unseason'd hours;
    And he is rich for it, an elder brother!
    His barns are full, his ricks and mows well trod,
    His garners crack with store! O, 'tis well; ha, ha, ha!
    A plague consume thee, and thy house!
SORD. O here, "St. Swithin's, the 15 day, variable weather, for the most
    part rain", good! "for the most part rain": why, it should rain forty
    days after, now, more or less, it was a rule held, afore I was able to
    hold a plough, and yet here are two days no rain; ha! it makes me
    muse. We'll see how the next month begins, if that be better. "August

1, 2, 3, and 4, days, rainy and blustering:" this is well now: "5, 6, 7, 8, and 9, rainy, with some thunder;" Ay marry, this is excellent; the other was false printed sure: "the 10 and 11, great store of rain"; O good, good, good, good, good! "the 12, 13, and 14 days, rain"; good still: "15, and 16, rain"; good still: "17 and 18, rain", good still: "19 and 20", good still, good still, good still, good still, good still! "21, some rain"; some rain! well, we must be patient, and attend the heaven's pleasure, would it were more though: "the 22, 23, great tempests of rain, thunder and lightning".

O good again, past expectation good!
I thank my blessed angel; never, never
Laid I [a] penny better out than this,
To purchase this dear book: not dear for price,
And yet of me as dearly prized as life,
Since in it is contain'd the very life,
Blood, strength, and sinews, of my happiness.
Blest be the hour wherein I bought this book;
His studies happy that composed the book,
And the man fortunate that sold the book!
Sleep with this charm, and be as true to me,
As I am joy'd and confident in thee
          [PUTS IT UP.
[ENTER A HIND, AND GIVES SORDIDO A PAPER TO READ.
MAC. Ha, ha, ha!
    Is not this good? Is not pleasing this?
    Ha, ha, ha! God pardon me! ha, ha!
    Is't possible that such a spacious villain
    Should live, and not be plagued? or lies be hid
    Within the wrinkled bosom of the world,
    Where Heaven cannot see him? S'blood! methinks

'Tis rare, and strange, that he should breathe and walk,
Feed with digestion, sleep, enjoy his health,
And, like a boisterous whale swallowing the poor,
Still swim in wealth and pleasure! is't not strange?
Unless his house and skin were thunder proof,
I wonder at it! Methinks, now, the hectic,
Gout, leprosy, or some such loath'd disease,
Might light upon him; of that fire from heaven
Might fall upon his barns; or mice and rats
Eat up his grain; or else that it might rot
Within the hoary ricks, even as it stands:
Methinks this might be well; and after all
The devil might come and fetch him. Ay, 'tis true!
Meantime he surfeits in prosperity,
And thou, in envy of him, gnaw'st thyself:
Peace, fool, get hence, and tell thy vexed spirit,
Wealth in this age will scarcely look on merit.
[RISES AND EXIT.

SORD. Who brought this same, sirrah?

HIND. Marry, sir, one of the justice's men; he says 'tis a precept, and all
their hands be at it.

SORD. Ay, and the prints of them stick in my flesh,
Deeper than in their letters: they have sent me
Pills wrapt in paper here, that, should I take them,
Would poison all the sweetness of my book,
And turn my honey into hemlock juice.
But I am wiser than to serve their precepts,
Or follow their prescriptions. Here's a device,
To charge me bring my grain unto the markets:
Ay, much! when I have neither barn nor garner,
Nor earth to hid it in, I'll bring 't; till then,
Each corn I send shall be as big as Paul's.

O, but (say some) the poor are like to starve.
Why, let 'em starve, what's that to me? are bees
Bound to keep life in drones and idle moths? no:
Why such are these that term themselves the poor,
Only because they would be pitied,
But are indeed a sort of lazy beggars,
Licentious rogues, and sturdy vagabonds,
Bred by the sloth of a fat plenteous year,
Like snakes in heat of summer, out of dung;
And this is all that these cheap times are good for:
Whereas a wholesome and penurious dearth
Purges the soil of such vile excrements,
And kills the vipers up.

HIND. O, but master,
Take heed they hear you not.

SORD. Why so?

HIND. They will exclaim against you.

SORD. Ay, their exclaims
Move me as much, as thy breath moves a mountain.
Poor worms, they hiss at me, whilst I at home
Can be contented to applaud myself,
To sit and clap my hands, and laugh, and leap,
Knocking my head against my roof, with joy
To see how plump my bags are, and my barns.
Sirrah, go hie you home, and bid your fellows
Get all their flails ready again I come.

HIND. I will, sir.

[EXIT.

SORD. I'll instantly set all my hinds to thrashing
Of a whole rick of corn, which I will hide
Under the ground; and with the straw thereof

I'll stuff the outsides of my other mows:
That done, I'll have them empty all my garners,
And in the friendly earth bury my store,
That, when the searchers come, they may suppose
All's spent, and that my fortunes were belied.
And to lend more opinion to my want,
And stop that many-mouthed vulgar dog,
Which else would still be baying at my door,
Each market-day I will be seen to buy
Part of the purest wheat, as for my household;
Where when it comes, it shall increase my heaps:
'Twill yield me treble gain at this dear time,
Promised in this dear book: I have cast all.
Till then I will not sell an ear, I'll hang first.
O, I shall make my prices as I list;
My house and I can feed on peas and barley.
What though a world of wretches starve the while;
He that will thrive must think no courses vile.

[EXIT.

COR. Now, signior, how approve you this? have the humourists exprest
themselves truly or no?

MIT. Yes, if it be well prosecuted, 'tis hitherto happy enough: but methinks
Macilente went hence too soon; he might have been made to stay,
and speak somewhat in reproof of Sordido's wretchedness now at
the last.

COR. O, no, that had been extremely improper; besides, he had continued
the scene too long with him, as 'twas, being in no more action.

MIT. You may inforce the length as a necessary reason; but for propriety,
the scene wou'd very well have borne it, in my judgment.

COR. O, worst of both; why, you mistake his humour utterly then.

MIT. How do I mistake it? Is it not envy?

COR. Yes, but you must understand, signior, he envies him not as he is a villain, a wolf in the commonwealth, but as he is rich and fortunate; for the true condition of envy is, 'dolor alienae felicitatis', to have our eyes continually fixed upon another man's prosperity that is, his chief happiness, and to grieve at that. Whereas, if we make his monstrous and abhorr'd actions our object, the grief we take then comes nearer the nature of hate than envy, as being bred out of a kind of contempt and loathing in ourselves.

MIT. So you'll infer it had been hate, not envy in him, to reprehend the humour of Sordido?

COR. Right, for what a man truly envies in another, he could always love and cherish in himself; but no man truly reprehends in another, what he loves in himself; therefore reprehension is out of his hate. And this distinction hath he himself made in a speech there, if you marked it, where he says, "I envy not this Buffone, but I hate him." Why might he not as well have hated Sordido as him?

COR. No, sir, there was subject for his envy in Sordido, his wealth: so was there not in the other. He stood possest of no one eminent gift, but a most odious and fiend-like disposition, that would turn charity itself into hate, much more envy, for the present.

MIT. You have satisfied me, sir. O, here comes the fool, and the jester again, methinks.

COR. 'Twere pity they should be parted, sir.

MIT. What bright-shining gallant's that with them? the knight they went to?

COR. No, sir, this is one monsieur Fastidious Brisk, otherwise called the fresh Frenchified courtier.

MIT. A humourist too?

COR. As humorous as quicksilver; do but observe him; the scene is the country still, remember.

63

ACT II

SCENE I.—THE COUNTRY; BEFORE PUNTARVOLO'S HOUSE.

ENTER FASTIDIOUS BRISK, CINEDO, CARLO BUFFONE, AND SOGLIARDO.

FAST. Cinedo, watch when the knight comes, and give us word.

CIN. I will, sir.

        [EXIT.

FAST. How lik'st thou my boy, Carlo?

CAR. O, well, well. He looks like a colonel of the Pigmies horse, or one of these motions in a great antique clock; he would shew well upon a haberdasher's stall, at a corner shop, rarely.

FAST. 'Sheart, what a damn'd witty rogue's this! How he confounds with his similes!

CAR. Better with similes than smiles: and whither were you riding now, signior?

FAST. Who, I? What a silly jest's that! Whither should I ride but to the court?

CAR. O, pardon me, sir, twenty places more; your hot-house, or your whore-house—

FAST. By the virtue of my soul, this knight dwells in Elysium here.

CAR. He's gone now, I thought he would fly out presently. These be our nimble-spirited catsos, that have their evasions at pleasure, will run over a bog like your wild Irish; no sooner started, but they'll leap from one thing to another, like a squirrel, heigh! dance and do tricks in their discourse, from fire to water, from water to air, from air to earth, as if their tongues did but e'en lick the four elements over, and away.

FAST. Sirrah, Carlo, thou never saw'st my gray hobby yet, didst thou?

CAR. No; have you such a one?

FAST. The best in Europe, my good villain, thou'lt say when thou seest him.

CAR. But when shall I see him?

FAST. There was a nobleman in the court offered me a hundred pound for him, by this light: a fine little fiery slave, he runs like a—oh, excellent, excellent!—with the very sound of the spur.

CAR. How! the sound of the spur?

FAST. O, it's your only humour now extant, sir; a good gingle, a good gingle.

CAR. S'blood! you shall see him turn morrice-dancer, he has got him bells, a good suit, and a hobby-horse.

SIG. Signior, now you talk of a hobby-horse, I know where one is will not be given for a brace of angels.

FAST. How is that, sir?

SOG. Marry, sir, I am telling this gentleman of a hobby-horse; it was my father's indeed, and though I say it—

CAR. That should not say it—on, on.

SOG. He did dance in it, with as good humour and as good regard as any man of his degree whatsoever, being no gentleman: I have danc'd in it myself too.

CAR. Not since the humour of gentility was upon you, did you?

SOG. Yes, once; marry, that was but to shew what a gentleman might do in a humour.

CAR. O, very good.

MIT. Why, this fellow's discourse were nothing but for the word humour.

COR. O bear with him; an he should lack matter and words too, 'twere pitiful.

SOG. Nay, look you, sir, there's ne'er a gentleman in the country has the like humours, for the hobby-horse, as I have; I have the method for the threading of the needle and all, the—

CAR. How, the method?

SOG. Ay, the leigerity for that, and the whighhie, and the daggers in the nose, and the travels of the egg from finger to finger, and all the humours incident to the quality. The horse hangs at home in my parlour. I'll keep it for a monument as long as I live, sure.

CAR. Do so; and when you die, 'twill be an excellent trophy to hang over your tomb.

SOG. Mass, and I'll have a tomb, now I think on't; 'tis but so much charges.

CAR. Best build it in your lifetime then, your heirs may hap to forget it else.

SOG. Nay, I mean so, I'll not trust to them.

CAR. No, for heirs and executors are grown damnable careless, 'specially since the ghosts of testators left walking.—How like you him, signior?

FAST. 'Fore heavens, his humour arrides me exceedingly.

CAR. Arrides you!

FAST. Ay, pleases me: a pox on't! I am so haunted at the court, and at my lodging, with your refined choice spirits, that it makes me clean of another garb, another sheaf, I know not how! I cannot frame me to your harsh vulgar phrase, 'tis against my genius.

Sog. Signior Carlo! [TAKES HIM ASIDE.

COR. This is right to that of Horace, "Dum vitant stulti vitia, in contraria currunt"; so this gallant labouring to avoid popularity, falls into a habit of affectation, ten thousand times hatefuller than the former.

CAR. [POINTING TO FASTIDIOUS.] Who, he? a gull, a fool, no salt in him i' the earth, man; he looks like a fresh salmon kept in a tub; he'll be spent shortly. His brain's lighter than his feather already, and his tongue more subject to lye, than that is to wag; he sleeps with a musk-cat every night, and walks all day hang'd in pomander chains for penance; he has his skin tann'd in civet, to make his complexion strong, and the sweetness of his youth lasting in the sense of his sweet lady; a good empty puff, he loves you well, signior.

SOG. There shall be no love lost, sir, I'll assure you.

FAST. [ADVANCING TO THEM.] Nay, Carlo, I am not happy in thy love, I see: pray thee suffer me to enjoy thy company a little, sweet mischief: by this air, I shall envy this gentleman's place in thy affections, if you be thus private, i'faith. ENTER CINEDO. How now! Is the knight arrived?

CIN. No, sir, but 'tis guess'd he will arrive presently, by his fore-runners.

FAST. His hounds! by Minerva, an excellent figure; a good boy.

CAR. You should give him a French crown for it; the boy would find two better figures in that, and a good figure of your bounty beside.

FAST. Tut, the boy wants no crowns.

CAR. No crown; speak in the singular number, and we'll believe you.

FAST. Nay, thou are so capriciously conceited now. Sirrah damnation, I have heard this knight Puntarvolo reported to be a gentleman of exceeding good humour, thou know'st him; prithee, how is his disposition? I never was so favoured of my stars, as to see him yet. Boy, do you look to the hobby?

CIN. Ay, sir, the groom has set him up. [AS CINEDO IS GOING OUT, SOGLIARDO TAKES HIM ASIDE.

FAST. 'Tis well: I rid out of my way of intent to visit him, and take knowledge of his—Nay, good Wickedness, his humour, his humour.

CAR. Why, he loves dogs, and hawks, and his wife well; he has a good riding face, and he can sit a great horse; he will taint a staff well at tile; when he is mounted he looks like the sign of the George, that's all I know; save, that instead of a dragon, he will brandish against a tree, and break his sword as confidently upon the knotty bark, as the other did upon the scales of the beast.

FAST. O, but this is nothing to that's delivered of him. They say he has dialogues and discourses between his horse, himself, and his dog;

and that he will court his own lady, as she were a stranger never encounter'd before.

CAR. Ay, that he will, and make fresh love to her every morning; this gentleman has been a spectator of it, Signior Insulso.

SOG. I am resolute to keep a page.—Say you, sir? [LEAPS FROM WHISPERING WITH CINEDO.

CAR. You have seen Signior Puntarvolo accost his lady?

SOG. O, ay, sir.

FAST. And how is the manner of it, prithee, good signior?

SOG. Faith, sir, in very good sort; he has his humours for it, sir; at first, (suppose he were now to come from riding or hunting, or so,) he has his trumpet to sound, and then the waiting-gentlewoman she looks out, and then he speaks, and then she speaks,—very pretty, i'faith, gentlemen.

FAST. Why, but do you remember no particulars, signior?

SOG. O, yes, sir, first, the gentlewoman, she looks out at the window.

CAR. After the trumpet has summon'd a parle, not before?

SOG. No, sir, not before; and then says he,—ha, ha, ha, ha!

CAR. What says he? be not rapt so.

SOG. Says he,—ha, ha, ha, ha!

FAST. Nay, speak, speak.

SOG. Ha, ha, ha!—says he, God save you, says he;—ha, ha!

CAR. Was this the ridiculous motive to all this passion?

SOG. Nay, that that comes after is,—ha, ha, ha, ha!

CAR. Doubtless he apprehends more than he utters, this fellow; or else— [A CRY OF HOUNDS WITHIN.

SOG. List, list, they are come from hunting; stand by, close under this terras, and you shall see it done better than I can show it.

CAR. So it had need, 'twill scarce poise the observation else.

SOG. Faith, I remember all, but the manner of it is quite out of my head.

FAST. O, withdraw, withdraw, it cannot be but a most pleasing object.
[THEY STAND ASIDE.
ENTER PUNTARVOLO, FOLLOWED BY HIS HUNTSMAN
LEADING A GREYHOUND. PUNT. Forester, give wind to thy
horn.—Enough; by this the sound hath touch'd the ears of the
inclos'd: depart, leave the dog, and take with thee what thou has
deserved, the horn and thanks.
[EXIT HUNTSMAN.
CAR. Ay, marry, there is some taste in this.
FAST. Is't not good?
SOG. Ah, peace; now above, now above! [A WAITING-
GENTLEWOMAN APPEARS AT THE WINDOW.
PUNT. Stay; mine eye hath, on the instant, through the bounty of the
window, received the form of a nymph. I will step forward three
paces; of the which, I will barely retire one; and, after some little
flexure of the knee, with an erected grace salute her; one, two, and
three! Sweet lady, God save you!
GENT. [ABOVE.] No, forsooth; I am but the waiting-gentlewoman.
CAR. He knew that before.
PUNT. Pardon me: 'humanum est errare'.
CAR. He learn'd that of his chaplain.
PUNT. To the perfection of compliment (which is the dial of the
thought, and guided by the sun of your beauties,) are required these
three specials; the gnomon, the puntilios, and the superficies: the
superficies is that we call place; the puntilios, circumstance; and the
gnomon, ceremony; in either of which, for a stranger to err, 'tis easy
and facile; and such am I.
CAR. True, not knowing her horizon, he must needs err; which I fear he
knows too well.
PUNT. What call you the lord of the castle, sweet face?
GENT. [ABOVE.] The lord of the castle is a knight, sir; signior
Puntarvolo.

69

PUNT. Puntarvolo! O—

CAR. Now must he ruminate.

FAST. Does the wench know him all this while, then?

CAR. O, do you know me, man? why, therein lies the syrup of the jest; it's a project, a designment of his own, a thing studied, and rehearst as ordinarily at his coming from hawking or hunting, as a jig after a play.

SOG. Ay, e'en like your jig, sir.

PUNT. 'Tis a most sumptuous and stately edifice! Of what years is the knight, fair damsel?

GENT. Faith, much about your years, sir.

PUNT. What complexion, or what stature bears he?

GENT. Of your stature, and very near upon your complexion.

PUNT. Mine is melancholy,—

CAR. So is the dog's, just.

PUNT. And doth argue constancy, chiefly in love. What are his endowments? is he courteous?

GENT. O, the most courteous knight in Christian land, sir.

PUNT. Is he magnanimous?

GENT. As the skin between your brows, sir.

PUNT. Is he bountiful?

CAR. 'Slud, he takes an inventory of his own good parts.

GENT. Bountiful! ay, sir, I would you should know it; the poor are served at his gate, early and late, sir.

PUNT. Is he learned?

GENT. O, ay, sir, he can speak the French and Italian.

PUNT. Then he has travelled?

GENT. Ay, forsooth, he hath been beyond seas once or twice.

CAR. As far as Paris, to fetch over a fashion, and come back again.

PUNT. Is he religious?

GENT. Religious! I know not what you call religious, but he goes to church, I am sure.

FAST. 'Slid, methinks these answers should offend him.

CAR. Tut, no; he knows they are excellent, and to her capacity that speaks them.

PUNT. Would I might but see his face!

CAR. She should let down a glass from the window at that word, and request him to look in't.

PUNT. Doubtless the gentleman is most exact, and absolutely qualified; doth the castle contain him?

GENT. No, sir, he is from home, but his lady is within.

PUNT. His lady! what, is she fair, splendidious, and amiable?

GENT. O, Lord, sir.

PUNT. Prithee, dear nymph, intreat her beauties to shine on this side of the building.

               [EXIT WAITING-GENTLEWOMAN FROM THE WINDOW.

CAR. That he may erect a new dial of compliment, with his gnomons and his puntilios.

FAST. Nay, thou art such another cynic now, a man had need walk uprightly before thee.

CAR. Heart, can any man walk more upright than he does? Look, look; as if he went in a frame, or had a suit of wainscot on: and the dog watching him, lest he should leap out on't.

FAST. O, villain!

CAR. Well, an e'er I meet him in the city, I'll have him jointed, I'll pawn him in Eastcheap, among the butchers, else.

FAST. Peace; who be these, Carlo?

ENTER SORDIDO AND FUNGOSO.

SORD. Yonder's your godfather; do your duty to him, son.

SOG. This, sir? a poor elder brother of mine, sir, a yeoman, may dispend some seven or eight hundred a year; that's his son, my nephew, there.

71

PUNT. You are not ill come, neighbour Sordido, though I have not yet said, well-come; what, my godson is grown a great proficient by this.

SORD. I hope he will grow great one day, sir.

FAST. What does he study? the law?

SOG. Ay, sir, he is a gentleman, though his father be but a yeoman.

CAR. What call you your nephew, signior?

SOG. Marry, his name is Fungoso.

CAR. Fungoso! O, he look'd somewhat like a sponge in that pink'd yellow doublet, methought; well, make much of him; I see he was never born to ride upon a mule.

GENT. [REAPPEARS AT THE WINDOW.] My lady will come presently, sir.

SOG. O, now, now!

PUNT. Stand by, retire yourselves a space; nay, pray you, forget not the use of your hat; the air is piercing. [SORDIDO AND FUNGOSO WITHDRAW.

FAST. What! will not their presence prevail against the current of his humour?

CAR. O, no; it's a mere flood, a torrent carries all afore it.

 [LADY PUNTARVOLO APPEARS AT THE WINDOW.

PUNT. What more than heavenly pulchritude is this.

 What magazine, or treasury of bliss?

 Dazzle, you organs to my optic sense,

 To view a creature of such eminence:

 O, I am planet-struck, and in yon sphere

 A brighter star than Venus doth appear!

FAST. How! in verse!

CAR. An extacy, an extacy, man.

LADY P. [ABOVE] is your desire to speak with me, sir knight?

CAR. He will tell you that anon; neither his brain nor his body are yet moulded for an answer.

PUNT. Most debonair, and luculent lady, I decline me as low as the basis of your altitude.

COR. He makes congies to his wife in geometrical proportions.

MIT. Is it possible there should be any such humorist?

COR. Very easily possible, sir, you see there is.

PUNT. I have scarce collected my spirits, but lately scattered in the administration of your form; to which, if the bounties of your mind be any way responsible, I doubt not but my desires shall find a smooth and secure passage. I am a poor knight-errant, lady, that hunting in the adjacent forest, was, by adventure, in the pursuit of a hart, brought to this place; which hart, dear madam, escaped by enchantment: the evening approaching myself and servant wearied, my suit is, to enter your fair castle and refresh me.

LADY. Sir knight, albeit it be not usual with me, chiefly in the absence of a husband, to admit any entrance to strangers, yet in the true regard of those innated virtues, and fair parts, which so strive to express themselves, in you; I am resolved to entertain you to the best of my unworthy power; which I acknowledge to be nothing, valued with what so worthy a person may deserve. Please you but stay while I descend.

[EXIT FROM THE WINDOW.

PUNT. Most admired lady, you astonish me. [WALKS ASIDE WITH SORDIDO AND HIS SON.

CAR. What! with speaking a speech of your own penning?

FAST. Nay, look: prithee, peace.

CAR. Pox on't! I am impatient of such foppery.

FAST. O let us hear the rest.

CAR. What! a tedious chapter of courtship, after sir Lancelot and queen Guenever? Away! I marle in what dull cold nook he found this lady out; that, being a woman, she was blest with no more copy of wit but to serve his humour thus. 'Slud, I think he feeds her with porridge, I: she could never have such a thick brain else.

SOG. Why, is porridge so hurtful, signior?

CAR. O, nothing under heaven more prejudicial to those ascending subtle powers, or doth sooner abate that which we call 'acumen ingenii', than your gross fare: Why, I'll make you an instance; your city-wives, but observe 'em, you have not more perfect true fools in the world bred than they are generally; and yet you see, by the fineness and delicacy of their diet, diving into the fat capons, drinking your rich wines, feeding on larks, sparrows, potato-pies, and such good unctuous meats, how their wits are refined and rarified; and sometimes a very quintessence of conceit flows from them, able to drown a weak apprehension.

ENTER LADY PUNTARVOLO AND HER WAITING-WOMAN. FAST. Peace, here comes the lady..

LADY. Gad's me, here's company! turn in again.
[EXIT WITH HER WOMAN.

FAST. 'Slight, our presence has cut off the convoy of the jest.

CAR. All the better, I am glad on't; for the issue was very perspicuous. Come let's discover, and salute the knight. [THEY COME FORWARD.

PUNT. Stay; who be these that address themselves towards us? What Carlo! Now by the sincerity of my soul, welcome; welcome, gentlemen: and how dost thou, thou 'Grand Scourge', or 'Second Untruss of the time'?

CAR. Faith, spending my metal in this reeling world (here and there), as the sway of my affection carries me, and perhaps stumble upon a yeoman-feuterer, as I do now; or one of fortune's mules, laden with treasure, and an empty cloak-bag, following him, gaping when a gab will untie.

PUNT. Peace, you bandog, peace! What brisk Nymphadoro is that in the white virgin-boot there?

74

CAR. Marry, sir, one that I must interest you to take a very particular knowledge of, and with more than ordinary respect; monsieur Fastidious.

PUNT. Sir, I could wish, that for the time of your vouchsafed abiding here, and more real entertainment, this is my house stood on the Muses hill, and these my orchards were those of the Hesperides.

FAST. I possess as much in your wish, sir, as if I were made lord of the Indies; and I pray you believe it.

CAR. I have a better opinion of his faith, than to think it will be so corrupted.

SOG. Come, brother, I'll bring you acquainted with gentlemen, and good fellows, such as shall do you more grace than—

SORD. Brother, I hunger not for such acquaintance: Do you take heed, lest—[CARLO COMES TOWARD THEM.

SOG. Husht! My brother, sir, for want of education, sir, somewhat nodding to the boor, the clown; but I request you in private, sir.

FUNG. [LOOKING AT FASTIDIOUS BRISK.] By heaven, it is a very fine suit of clothes. [ASIDE.

COR. Do you observe that signior? There's another humour has new-crack'd the shell.

MIT. What! he is enamour'd of the fashion, is he?

COR. O, you forestall the jest.

FUNG. I marle what it might stand him in. [ASIDE.

SOG. Nephew!

FUNG. 'Fore me, it's an excellent suit, and as neatly becomes him. [ASIDE.]—What said you, uncle?

SOG. When saw you my niece?

FUNG. Marry, yesternight I supp'd there.—That kind of boot does very rare too. [ASIDE.

SOG. And what news hear you?

FUNG. The gilt spur and all! Would I were hang'd, but 'tis exceeding good. [ASIDE.]—Say you, uncle?

SOG. Your mind is carried away with somewhat else: I ask what news you hear?

FUNG. Troth, we hear none.—In good faith [LOOKING AT FASTIDIOUS BRISK] I was never so pleased with a fashion, days of my life. O an I might have but my wish, I'd ask no more of heaven now, but such a suit, such a hat, such a band, such a doublet, such a hose, such a boot, and such a—[ASIDE.

SOG. They say, there's a new motion of the city of Nineveh, with Jonas and the whale, to be seen at Fleet-bridge. You can tell, cousin?

FUNG. Here's such a world of questions with him now!—Yes, I think there be such a thing, I saw the picture.—Would he would once be satisfied! Let me see, the doublet, say fifty shillings the doublet, and between three or four pound the hose; then boots, hat, and band: some ten or eleven pound will do it all, and suit me for the heavens! [ASIDE.

SOG. I'll see all those devices an I come to London once.

FUNG. Ods 'slid, an I could compass it, 'twere rare [ASIDE.]—Hark you, uncle.

SOG. What says my nephew?

FUNG. Faith, uncle, I would have desired you to have made a motion for me to my father, in a thing that—Walk aside, and I'll tell you, sir; no more but this: there's a parcel of law books (some twenty pounds worth) that lie in a place for a little more than half the money they cost; and I think, for some twelve pound, or twenty mark, I could go near to redeem them; there's Plowden, Dyar, Brooke, and Fitz-Herbert, divers such as I must have ere long; and you know, I were as good save five or six pound, as not, uncle. I pray you, move it for me.

SOG. That I will: when would you have me do it? presently?

FUNG. O, ay, I pray you, good uncle: [SOGLIARDO TAKES SORDIDO ASIDE.]—send me good luck, Lord, an't be thy will, prosper it! O my stars, now, now, if it take now, I am made for ever.

FAST. Shall I tell you, sir? by this air, I am the most beholden to that lord, of any gentleman living; he does use me the most honourably, and with the greatest respect, more indeed than can be utter'd with any opinion of truth.

PUNT. Then have you the count Gratiato?

FAST. As true noble a gentleman too as any breathes; I am exceedingly endear'd to his love: By this hand, I protest to you, signior, I speak it not gloriously, nor out of affectation, but there's he and the count Frugale, signior Illustre, signior Luculento, and a sort of 'em, that when I am at court, they do share me amongst them; happy is he can enjoy me most private. I do wish myself sometime an ubiquitary for their love, in good faith.

CAR. There's ne'er a one of them but might lie a week on the rack, ere they could bring forth his name; and yet he pours them out as familiarly, as if he had seen them stand by the fire in the presence, or ta'en tobacco with them over the stage, in the lord's room.

PUNT. Then you must of necessity know our court-star there, that planet of wit, madona Saviolina?

FAST. O Lord, sir, my mistress.

PUNT. Is she your mistress?

FAST. Faith, here be some slight favours of hers, sir, that do speak it, she is; as this scarf, sir, or this ribbon in my ear, or so; this feather grew in her sweet fan sometimes, though now it be my poor fortune to wear it, as you see, sir: slight, slight, a foolish toy.

PUNT. Well, she is the lady of a most exalted and ingenious spirit.

FAST. Did you ever hear any woman speak like her? or enriched with a more plentiful discourse?

CAR. O villainous! nothing but sound, sound, a mere echo; she speaks as she goes tired, in cobweb-lawn, light, thin; good enough to catch flies withal.

PUNT. O manage your affections.

FAST. Well, if thou be'st not plagued for this blasphemy one day—

77

PUNT. Come, regard not a jester: It is in the power of my purse to make him speak well or ill of me.

FAST. Sir, I affirm it to you upon my credit and judgment, she has the most harmonious and musical strain of wit that ever tempted a true ear; and yet to see!—a rude tongue would profane heaven, if it could.

PUNT. I am not ignorant of it, sir.

FAST. Oh, it flows from her like nectar, and she doth give it that sweet quick grace, and exornation in the composure that by this good air, as I am an honest man, would I might never stir, sir, but—she does observe as pure a phrase, and use as choice figures in her ordinary conferences, as any be in the 'Arcadia'.

CAR. Or rather in Green's works, whence she may steal with more security.

SORD. Well, if ten pound will fetch 'em, you shall have it; but I'll part with no more.

FUNG. I'll try what that will do, if you please.

SORD. Do so; and when you have them, study hard.

FUNG. Yes, sir. An I could study to get forty shillings more now! Well, I will put myself into the fashion, as far as this will go, presently.

SORD. I wonder it rains not: the almanack says, we should have a store of rain today. [ASIDE.

PUNT. Why, sir, tomorrow I will associate you to court myself, and from thence to the city about a business, a project I have; I will expose it to you sir; Carlo, I am sure has heard of it.

CAR. What's that, sir?

PUNT. I do intend, this year of jubilee coming on, to travel: and because I will not altogether go upon expense, I am determined to put forth some five thousand pound, to be paid me five for one, upon the return of myself, my wife, and my dog from the Turk's court in Constantinople. If all or either of us miscarry in the journey, 'tis gone: if we be successful, why, there will be five and twenty thousand pound to entertain time withal. Nay, go not, neighbour Sordido; stay tonight, and help to make our society the fuller. Gentlemen, frolic: Carlo! what! dull now?

CAR. I was thinking on your project, sir, an you call it so. Is this the dog goes with you?

PUNT. This is the dog, sir.

CAR. He does not go barefoot, does he?

PUNT. Away, you traitor, away!

CAR. Nay, afore God, I speak simply; he may prick his foot with a thorn, and be as much as the whole venture is worth. Besides, for a dog that never travell'd before, it's a huge journey to Constantinople. I'll tell you now, an he were mine, I'd have some present conference with a physician, what antidotes were good to give him, preservatives against poison; for assure you, if once your money be out, there'll be divers attempts made against the life of the poor animal.

PUNT. Thou art still dangerous.

FAST. Is signior Deliro's wife your kinswoman?

SOG. Ay, sir, she is my niece, my brother's daughter here, and my nephew's sister.

SORD. Do you know her, sir?

FAST. O Lord, sir! signior Deliro, her husband, is my merchant.

FUNG. Ay, I have seen this gentleman there often.

FAST. I cry you mercy, sir; let me crave your name, pray you.

FUNG. Fungoso, sir.

FAST. Good signior Fungoso, I shall request to know you better, sir.

FUNG. I am her brother, sir.

FAST. In fair time, sir.

PUNT. Come, gentlemen, I will be your conduct.

FAST. Nay, pray you sir; we shall meet at signior Deliro's often.

SOG. You shall have me at the herald's office, sir, for some week or so at my first coming up. Come, Carlo. [EXEUNT.

MIT. Methinks, Cordatus, he dwelt somewhat too long on this scene; it hung in the hand.

COR. I see not where he could have insisted less, and to have made the humours perspicuous enough.

MIT. True, as his subject lies; but he might have altered the shape of his argument, and explicated them better in single scenes.

COR. That had been single indeed. Why, be they not the same persons in this, as they would have been in those? and is it not an object of more state, to behold the scene full, and relieved with variety of speakers to the end, than to see a vast empty stage, and the actors come in one by one, as if they were dropt down with a feather into the eye of the spectators?

MIT. Nay, you are better traded with these things than I, and therefore I'll subscribe to your judgment; marry, you shall give me leave to make objections.

COR. O, what else? it is the special intent of the author you should do so; for thereby others, that are present, may as well be satisfied, who haply would object the same you would do.

MIT. So, sir; but when appears Macilente again?

COR. Marry, he stays but till our silence give him leave: here he comes, and with him signior Deliro, a merchant at whose house he is come to sojourn: make your own observation now, only transfer your thoughts to the city, with the scene: where suppose they speak.

SCENE II. A ROOM IN DELIRO'S HOUSE.

ENTER DELIRO, MACILENTE, AND FIDO WITH FLOWERS AND PERFUMES.

DELI. I'll tell you by and by, sir,—
Welcome good Macilente, to my house,

To sojourn even for ever; if my best in cates, and every sort of
   good entreaty,
May move you stay with me.

[HE CENSETH: THE BOY STREWS FLOWERS.

MACI. I thank you, sir.—
   And yet the muffled Fates, had it pleased them,
   Might have supplied me from their own full store.
   Without this word, 'I thank you', to a fool.
   I see no reason why that dog call'd Chance,
   Should fawn upon this fellow more than me;
   I am a man, and I have limbs, flesh, blood,
   Bones, sinews, and a soul, as well as he:
   My parts are every way as good as his;
   If I said better, why, I did not lie.
   Nath'less, his wealth, but nodding on my wants,
   Must make me bow, and cry, 'I thank you, sir'.
   [ASIDE.
DELI. Dispatch! take heed your mistress see you not.
FIDO. I warrant you, sir, I'll steal by her softly.

[EXIT.
DELI. Nay, gentle friend, be merry; raise your looks
   Out of your bosom: I protest, by heaven,
   You are the man most welcome in the world.
MACI. I thank you, sir.—I know my cue, I think.
   [ASIDE.
   RE-ENTER FIDO, WITH MORE PERFUMES AND
   FLOWERS.
FIDO. Where will you have them burn, sir?
DELI. Here, good Fido.

What, she did not see thee?

FIDO. No, sir.

DELI. That is well

Strew, strew, good Fido, the freshest flowers; so!

MACI. What means this, signior Deliro? all this censing?

DELI. Cast in more frankincense, yet more; well said.—

O Macilente, I have such a wife!

So passing fair! so passing-fair-unkind!

But of such worth, and right to be unkind,

Since no man can be worthy of her kindness—

MACI. What, can there not?

DELI. No, that is as sure as death,

No man alive. I do not say, is not,

But cannot possibly be worth her kindness,

Nay, it is certain, let me do her right.

How, said I? do her right! as though I could,

As though this dull, gross tongue of mine could utter

The rare, the true, the pure, the infinite rights.

That sit, as high as I can look, within her!

MACI. This is such dotage as was never heard.

DELI. Well, this must needs be granted.

MACI. Granted, quoth you?

DELI. Nay, Macilente, do not so discredit

The goodness of your judgment to deny it.

For I do speak the very least of her:

And I would crave, and beg no more of Heaven,

For all my fortunes here, but to be able

To utter first in fit terms, what she is,

And then the true joys I conceive in her.

MACI. Is't possible she should deserve so well,

As you pretend?

DELI. Ay, and she knows so well

Her own deserts, that, when I strive t'enjoy them,
She weighs the things I do, with what she merits;
And, seeing my worth out-weigh'd so in her graces,
She is so solemn, so precise, so froward,
That no observance I can do to her
Can make her kind to me: if she find fault,
I mend that fault; and then she says, I faulted,
That I did mend it. Now, good friend, advise me,
How I may temper this strange spleen in her.

MACI. You are too amorous, too obsequious,
    And make her too assured she may command you.
    When women doubt most of their husbands' loves,
    They are most loving. Husbands must take heed
    They give no gluts of kindness to their wives,
    But use them like their horses; whom they feed
    But half a peck at once; and keep them so
    Still with an appetite to that they give them.
    He that desires to have a loving wife,
    Must bridle all the show of that desire:
    Be kind, not amorous; nor bewraying kindness,
    As if love wrought it, but considerate duty.
    Offer no love rites, but let wives still seek them,
    For when they come unsought, they seldom like them.

DELI. Believe me, Macilente, this is gospel.
    O, that a man were his own man so much,
    To rule himself thus. I will strive, i'faith,
    To be more strange and careless; yet I hope
    I have now taken such a perfect course,
    To make her kind to me, and live contented,
    That I shall find my kindness well return'd,
    And have no need to fight with my affections.
    She late hath found much fault with every room

Within my house; one was too big, she said,
Another was not furnish'd to her mind,
And so through all; all which, now, I have alter'd.
Then here, she hath a place, on my back-side,
Wherein she loves to walk; and that, she said,
Had some ill smells about it: now, this walk
Have I before she knows it, thus perfumed
With herbs, and flowers; and laid in divers places,
As 'twere on altars consecrate to her,
Perfumed gloves, and delicate chains of amber,
To keep the air in awe of her sweet nostrils:
This have I done, and this I think will please her.
Behold, she comes.

ENTER FALLACE.

FAL. Here's a sweet stink indeed!
    What, shall I ever be thus crost and plagued,
    And sick of husband? O, my head doth ache,
    As it would cleave asunder, with these savours!
    All my rooms alter'd, and but one poor walk
    That I delighted in, and that is made
    So fulsome with perfumes, that I am fear'd,
    My brain doth sweat so, I have caught the plague!
DELI. Why, gentle wife, is now thy walk too sweet?
    Thou said'st of late, it had sour airs about it,
    And found'st much fault that I did not correct it.
FAL. Why, an I did find fault, sir?
DELI. Nay, dear wife,
    I know thou hast said thou has loved perfumes,
    No woman better.
FAL. Ay, long since, perhaps;

84

But now that sense is alter'd: you would have me,
Like to a puddle, or a standing pool,
To have no motion nor no spirit within me.
No. I am like a pure and sprightly river,
That moves for ever, and yet still the same;
Or fire, that burns much wood, yet still one flame.

DELI. But yesterday, I saw thee at our garden,
  Smelling on roses, and on purple flowers;
  And since, I hope, the humour of thy sense
  Is nothing changed.

FAL. Why, those were growing flowers,
  And these within my walk are cut and strewed.

DELI. But yet they have one scent.

FAL. Ay! have they so?
  In your gross judgment. If you make no difference
  Betwixt the scent of growing flowers and cut ones,
  You have a sense to taste lamp oil, i'faith:
  And with such judgment have you changed the chambers,
  Leaving no room, that I can joy to be in,
  In all your house; and now my walk, and all,
  You smoke me from, as if I were a fox,
  And long, belike, to drive me quite away:
  Well, walk you there, and I'll walk where I list.

DELI. What shall I do? O, I shall never please her.

MACI. Out on thee, dotard! what star ruled his birth,
  That brought him such a Star? blind Fortune still
  Bestows her gifts on such as cannot use them:
  How long shall I live, ere I be so happy
  To have a wife of this exceeding form?
  [ASIDE.

DELI. Away with 'em! would I had broke a joint
  When I devised this, that should so dislike her.

85

Away, bear all away.

[EXIT FIDO, WITH FLOWERS, ETC.

FAL. Ay, do; for fear
    Aught that is there should like her. O, this man,
    How cunningly he can conceal himself,
    As though he loved, nay, honour'd and ador'd!—
DELI. Why, my sweet heart?
FAL. Sweet heart! O, better still!
    And asking, why? wherefore? and looking strangely,
    As if he were as white as innocence!
    Alas, you're simple, you: you cannot change,
    Look pale at pleasure, and then red with wonder;
    No, no, not you! 'tis pity o' your naturals.
    I did but cast an amorous eye, e'en now,
    Upon a pair of gloves that somewhat liked me,
    And straight he noted it, and gave command
    All should be ta'en away.
DELI. Be they my bane then!
    What, sirrah, Fido, bring in those gloves again
    You took from hence.
FAL. 'Sbody, sir, but do not:
    Bring in no gloves to spite me; if you do—
DELI. Ay me, most wretched; how am I misconstrued!
MACI. O, how she tempts my heart-strings with her eye,
    To knit them to her beauties, or to break!
    What mov'd the heavens, that they could not make
    Me such a woman! but a man, a beast,
    That hath no bliss like others? Would to heaven,
    In wreak of my misfortunes, I were turn'd
    To some fair water-nymph, that set upon
    The deepest whirl-pit of the rav'nous seas,

My adamantine eyes might headlong hale
This iron world to me, and drown it all.
　　[ASIDE.
COR. Behold, behold, the translated gallant.
MIT. O, he is welcome.
　　ENTER FUNGOSO, APPARELLED LIKE FASTIDIOUS
　　BRISK. FUNG. Save you, brother and sister; save you, sir! I have
　　commendations for you out o' the country. I wonder they take no
　　knowledge of my suit: [ASIDE.]—Mine uncle Sogliardo is in town.
　　Sister methinks you are melancholy; why are you so sad? I think you
　　took me for Master Fastidious Brisk, sister, did you not?
FAL. Why should I take you for him?
FUNG. Nay, nothing.—I was lately in Master Fastidious's company, and
　　methinks we are very like.
DELI. You have a fair suit, brother, 'give you joy on't.
FUNG. Faith, good enough to ride in, brother; I made it to ride in.
FAL. O, now I see the cause of his idle demand was his new suit.
DELI. Pray you, good brother, try if you can change her mood.
FUNG. I warrant you, let me alone: I'll put her out of her dumps. Sister,
　　how like you my suit!
FAL. O, you are a gallant in print now, brother.
FUNG. Faith, how like you the fashion? it is the last edition, I assure
　　you.
FAL. I cannot but like it to the desert.
FUNG. Troth, sister, I was fain to borrow these spurs, I have left my
　　gown in the gage for them, pray you lend me an angel.
FAL. Now, beshrew my heart then.
FUNG. Good truth, I'll pay you again at my next exhibition. I had but
　　bare ten pound of my father, and it would not reach to put me
　　wholly into the fashion.
FAL. I care not.

FUNG. I had spurs of mine own before, but they were not ginglers.
   Monsieur Fastidious will be here anon, sister.

FAL. You jest!

FUNG. Never lend me penny more while you live then; and that I'd be
   loth to say, in truth.

FAL. When did you see him?

FUNG. Yesterday; I came acquainted with him at Sir Puntarvolo's: nay,
   sweet sister.

MACI. I fain would know of heaven now, why yond fool
   Should wear a suit of satin? he? that rook,
   That painted jay, with such a deal of outside:
   What is his inside, trow? ha, ha, ha, ha, ha!
   Good heavens, give me patience, patience, patience.
   A number of these popinjays there are,
   Whom, if a man confer, and but examine
   Their inward merit, with such men as want;
   Lord, lord, what things they are!
   [ASIDE.

FAL. [GIVES HIM MONEY.] Come, when will you pay me again,
   now?

FUNG. O lord, sister!

MACI. Here comes another.

ENTER FASTIDIOUS BRISK, IN A NEW SUIT. FAST. Save you,
   signior Deliro! How dost thou, sweet lady? let me kiss thee.

FUNG. How! a new suit? ah me!

DELI. And how does master Fastidious Brisk?

FAST. Faith, live in court, signior Deliro; in grace, I thank God, both of
   the noble masculine and feminine. I muse speak with you in private
   by and by.

DELI. When you please, sir.

FAL. Why look you so pale, brother?

FUNG. 'Slid, all this money is cast away now.

MACI. Ay, there's a newer edition come forth.

FUNG. 'Tis but my hard fortune! well, I'll have my suit changed. I'll go fetch my tailor presently but first, I'll devise a letter to my father. Have you any pen and ink, sister?

FAL. What would you do withal?

FUNG. I would use it. 'Slight, an it had come but four days sooner, the fashion.

[EXIT.

FAST. There was a countess gave me her hand to kiss today, i' the presence: did me more good by that light than—and yesternight sent her coach twice to my lodging, to intreat me accompany her, and my sweet mistress, with some two or three nameless ladies more: O, I have been graced by them beyond all aim of affection: this is her garter my dagger hangs in: and they do so commend and approve my apparel, with my judicious wearing of it, it's above wonder.

FAL. Indeed, sir, 'tis a most excellent suit, and you do wear it as extraordinary.

FAST. Why, I'll tell you now, in good faith, and by this chair, which, by the grace of God, I intend presently to sit in, I had three suits in one year made three great ladies in love with me: I had other three, undid three gentlemen in imitation: and other three gat three other gentlemen widows of three thousand pound a year.

DELI. Is't possible?

FAST. O, believe it, sir; your good face is the witch, and your apparel the spells, that bring all the pleasures of the world into their circle.

FAL. Ah, the sweet grace of a courtier!

MACI. Well, would my father had left me but a good face for my portion yet! though I had shared the unfortunate with that goes with it, I had not cared; I might have passed for somewhat in the world then.

FAST. Why, assure you, signior, rich apparel has strange virtues: it makes him that hath it without means, esteemed for an excellent wit: he that enjoys it with means, puts the world in remembrance of his means: it helps the deformities of nature, and gives lustre to her beauties; makes continual holiday where it shines; sets the wits of ladies at work, that otherwise would be idle; furnisheth your two-shilling ordinary; takes possession of your stage at your new play; and enricheth your oars, as scorning to go with your scull.

MACI. Pray you, sir, add this; it gives respect to your fools, makes many thieves, as many strumpets, and no fewer bankrupts.

FAL. Out, out! unworthy to speak where he breatheth.

FAST. What's he, signior?

DELI. A friend of mine, sir.

FAST. By heaven I wonder at you citizens, what kind of creatures you are!

DELI. Why, sir?

FAST. That you can consort yourselves with such poor seam-rent fellows.

FAL. He says true.

DELI. Sir, I will assure you, however you esteem of him, he's a man worthy of regard.

FAST. Why, what has he in him of such virtue to be regarded, ha?

DELI. Marry, he is a scholar, sir.

FAST. Nothing else!

DELI. And he is well travell'd.

FAST. He should get him clothes; I would cherish those good parts of travel in him, and prefer him to some nobleman of good place.

DELI. Sir, such a benefit should bine me to you for ever, in my friend's right; and I doubt not, but his desert shall more than answer my praise.

FAST. Why, an he had good clothes, I'd carry him to court with me tomorrow.

DELI. He shall not want for those, sir, if gold and the whole city will furnish him.

90

FAST. You say well, sir: faith, signior Deliro, I am come to have you play the alchemist with me, and change the species of my land into that metal you talk of.

DELI. With all my heart, sir; what sum will serve you?

FAST. Faith, some three or four hundred.

DELI. Troth, sir, I have promised to meet a gentleman this morning in Paul's, but upon my return I'll dispatch you.

FAST. I'll accompany you thither.

DELI. As you please, sir; but I go not thither directly.

FAST. 'Tis no matter, I have no other designment in hand, and therefore as good go along.

DELI. I were as good have a quartain fever follow me now, for I shall ne'er be rid of him. Bring me a cloak there, one. Still, upon his grace at court, I am sure to be visited; I was a beast to give him any hope. Well, would I were in, that I am out with him once, and—Come, signior Macilente, I must confer with you, as we go. Nay, dear wife, I beseech thee, forsake these moods: look not like winter thus. Here, take my keys, open my counting-houses, spread all my wealth before thee, choose any object that delights thee: if thou wilt eat the spirit of gold, and drink dissolved pearl in wine, 'tis for thee.

FAL. So, sir!

DELI. Nay, my sweet wife.

FAL. Good lord, how you are perfumed in your terms and all! pray you leave us.

DELI. Come, gentlemen.

FAST. Adieu, sweet lady. [EXEUNT ALL BUT FALLACE.

FAL. Ay, ay! let thy words ever sound in mine ears, and thy graces disperse contentment through all my senses! O, how happy is that lady above other ladies, that enjoys so absolute a gentleman to her servant! "A countess gives him her hand to kiss": ah, foolish countess! he's a man worthy, if a woman may speak of a man's worth, to kiss the lips of an empress.

RE-ENTER FUNGOSO, WITH HIS TAILOR. FUNG. What's master Fastidious gone, sister?

FAL. Ay, brother.—He has a face like a cherubin! [ASIDE.

FUNG. 'Ods me, what luck's this? I have fetch'd my tailor and all: which way went he, sister, can you tell?

FAL. Not I, in good faith—and he has a body like an angel! [ASIDE.

FUNG. How long is't since he went?

FAL. Why, but e'en now; did you not meet him?—and a tongue able to ravish any woman in the earth. [ASIDE.

FUNG. O, for God's sake—I'll please you for your pains, [TO HIS TAILOR.]—But e'en now, say you? Come, good sir: 'slid, I had forgot it too: if any body ask for mine uncle Sogliardo, they shall have him at the herald's office yonder, by Paul's

[EXIT WITH HIS TAILOR.

FAL. Well, I will not altogether despair: I have heard of a citizen's wife has been beloved of a courtier; and why not I? heigh, ho! well, I will into my private chamber, lock the door to me, and think over all his good parts one after another.

[EXIT.

MIT. Well, I doubt, this last scene will endure some grievous torture.

COR. How? you fear 'twill be rack'd by some hard construction?

MIT. Do not you?

COR. No, in good faith: unless mine eyes could light me beyond sense. I see no reason why this should be more liable to the rack than the rest: you'll say, perhaps, the city will not take it well that the merchant is made here to doat so perfectly upon his wife; and she again to be so 'Fastidiously' affected as she is.

MIT. You have utter'd my thought, sir, indeed.

COR. Why, by that proportion, the court might as well take offence at him we call the courtier, and with much more pretext, by how much the place transcends, and goes before in dignity and virtue: but can you imagine that any noble or true spirit in court, whose sinewy and altogether unaffected graces, very worthily express him a courtier, will make any exception at the opening of such as empty trunk as this Brisk is? or think his own worth impeached, by beholding his motley inside?

MIT. No, sir, I do not.

COR. No more, assure you, will any grave, wise citizen, or modest matron, take the object of this folly in Deliro and his wife; but rather apply it as the foil to their own virtues. For that were to affirm, that a man writing of Nero, should mean all emperors; or speaking of Machiavel, comprehend all statesmen; or in our Sordido, all farmers; and so of the rest: than which nothing can be uttered more malicious or absurd. Indeed there are a sort of these narrow-eyed decypherers, I confess, that will extort strange and abstruse meanings out of any subject, be it never so conspicuous and innocently delivered. But to such, where'er they sit concealed, let them know, the author defies them and their writing-tables; and hopes no sound or safe judgment will infect itself with their contagious comments, who, indeed, come here only to pervert and poison the sense of what they hear, and for nought else.

ENTER CAVALIER SHIFT, WITH TWO SI-QUISSES (BILLS) IN HIS HAND. MIT. Stay, what new mute is this, that walks so suspiciously?

COR. O, marry, this is one, for whose better illustration, we must desire you to presuppose the stage, the middle aisle in Paul's, and that, the west end of it.

MIT. So, sir, and what follows?

COR. Faith, a whole volume of humour, and worthy the unclasping.

MIT. As how? What name do you give him first?

COR. He hath shift of names, sir: some call him Apple-John, some signior Whiffe; marry, his main standing name is cavalier Shirt: the rest are but as clean shirts to his natures.

MIT. And what makes he in Paul's now?

COR. Troth, as you see, for the advancement of a 'si quis', or two; wherein he has so varied himself, that if any of 'em take, he may hull up and down in the humorous world a little longer.

MIT. It seems then he bears a very changing sail?

COR. O, as the wind, sir: here comes more.

ACT III

SCENE I.—THE MIDDLE AISLE OF ST. PAUL'S.

SHIFT. [COMING FORWARD.] This is rare, I have set up my bills without discovery.

[ENTER ORANGE. ORANGE. What, signior Whiffe! what fortune has brought you into these west parts?

SHIFT. Troth, signior, nothing but your rheum; I have been taking an ounce of tobacco hard by here, with a gentleman, and I am come to spit private in Paul's. 'Save you, sir.

ORANGE. Adieu, good signior Whiffe. [PASSES ONWARD.

[ENTER CLOVE. CLOVE. Master Apple-John! you are well met; when shall we sup together, and laugh, and be fat with those good wenches, ha?

SHIFT. Faith, sir, I must now leave you, upon a few humours and occasions; but when you please, sir.

[EXIT.

CLOVE. Farewell, sweet Apple-John! I wonder there are no more store of gallants here.

MIT. What be these two, signior?

COR. Marry, a couple, sir, that are mere strangers to the whole scope of our play; only come to walk a turn or two in this scene of Paul's, by chance.

ORANGE. Save you, good master Clove!

94

CLOVE. Sweet master Orange.

MIT. How! Clove and Orange?

COR. Ay, and they are well met, for 'tis as dry an Orange as ever grew: nothing but salutation, and "O lord, sir!" and "It pleases you to say so, sir!" one that can laugh at a jest for company with a most plausible and extemporal grade; and some hour after in private ask you what it was. The other monsieur, Clove, is a more spiced youth; he will sit you a whole afternoon sometimes in a bookseller's shop, reading the Greek, Italian, and Spanish, when he understands not a word of either; if he had the tongues to his suits, he were an excellent linguist.

CLOVE. Do you hear this reported for certainty?

ORANGE. O lord, sir.

[ENTER PUNTARVOLO AND CARLO, FOLLOWED BY TWO SERVING-MEN, ONE LEADING A DOG, THE OTHER BEARING A BAG.

PUNT. Sirrah, take my cloak; and you, sir knave, follow me closer. If thou losest my dog, thou shalt die a dog's death; I will hang thee.

CAR. Tut, fear him not, he's a good lean slave; he loves a dog well, I warrant him; I see by his looks, I:—Mass, he's somewhat like him. 'Slud [TO THE SERVANT.] poison him, make him away with a crooked pin, or somewhat, man; thou may'st have more security of thy life; and—So sir; what! you have not put out your whole venture yet, have you?

PUNT. No, I do want yet some fifteen or sixteen hundred pounds; but my lady, my wife, is 'Out of her Humour', she does not now go.

CAR. No! how then?

PUNT. Marry, I am now enforced to give it out, upon the return of myself, my dog, and my cat.

CAR. Your cat! where is she?

PUNT. My squire has her there, in the bag; sirrah, look to her. How lik'st thou my change, Carlo?

95

CAR. Oh, for the better, sir; your cat has nine lives, and your wife has but one.

PUNT. Besides, she will never be sea-sick, which will save me so much in conserves. When saw you signior Sogliardo?

CAR. I came from him but now; he is at the herald's office yonder; he requested me to go afore, and take up a man or two for him in Paul's, against his cognisance was ready.

PUNT. What, has he purchased arms, then?

CAR. Ay, and rare ones too; of as many colours as e'er you saw any fool's coat in your life. I'll go look among yond' bills, an I can fit him with legs to his arms.

PUNT. With legs to his arms! Good! I will go with you, sir. [THEY GO TO READ THE BILLS.

ENTER FASTIDIOUS, DELIRO, AND MACILENTE. FAST. Come, let's walk in Mediterraneo: I assure you, sir, I am not the least respected among ladies; but let that pass: do you know how to go into the presence, sir?

MACI. Why, on my feet, sir.

FAST. No, on your head, sir; for 'tis that must bear you out, I assure you; as thus, sir. You must first have an especial care so to wear your hat, that it oppress not confusedly this your predominant, or foretop; because, when you come at the presence-door, you may with once or twice stroking up your forehead, thus, enter with your predominant perfect; that is, standing up stiff.

MACI. As if one were frighted?

FAST. Ay, sir.

MACI. Which, indeed, a true fear of your mistress should do, rather than gum-water, or whites of eggs; is't not so, sir?

FAST. An ingenious observation. Give me leave to crave your name, sir?

DELI. His name is Macilente, sir.

FAST. Good signior Macilente, if this gentleman, signior Deliro, furnish you, as he says he will, with clothes, I will bring you, tomorrow by this time, into the presence of the most divine and acute lady in court; you shall see sweet silent rhetorick, and dumb eloquence speaking in her eye, but when she speaks herself, such an anatomy of wit, so sinewised and arterised, that 'tis the goodliest model of pleasure that ever was to behold. Oh! she strikes the world into admiration of her; O, O, O! I cannot express them, believe me.

MACI. O, your only admiration is your silence, sir.

PUNT. 'Fore God, Carlo, this is good! let's read them again. [READS THE BILL. "If there be any lady or gentlewoman of good carriage that is desirous to entertain to her private uses, a young, straight, and upright gentleman, of the age of five or six and twenty at the most; who can serve in the nature of a gentleman-usher, and hath little legs of purpose, and a black satin suit of his own, to go before her in; which suit, for the more sweetening, now lies in lavender; and can hide his face with her fan, if need require; or sit in the cold at the stair foot for her, as well as another gentleman: let her subscribe her name and place, and diligent respect shall be given."

PUNT. This is above measure excellent, ha!

CAR. No, this, this! here's a fine slave. [READS. "If this city, or the suburbs of the same, do afford any young gentleman of the first, second, or third head, more or less, whose friends are but lately deceased, and whose lands are but new come into his hands, that, to be as exactly qualified as the best of our ordinary gallants are, is affected to entertain the most gentleman-like use of tobacco; as first, to give it the most exquisite perfume; then, to know all the delicate sweet forms for the assumption of it; as also the rare corollary and practice of the Cuban ebolition, euripus and whiff, which he shall receive or take in here at London, and evaporate at Uxbridge, or farther, if it please him. If there be any such generous spirit, that is truly enamoured of these good faculties; may it please him, but by a note of his hand to specify the place or ordinary where he uses to eat and lie; and most sweet attendance, with tobacco and pipes of the best sort, shall be ministered. 'Stet, quaeso, candide Lector.'"

PUNT. Why, this is without parallel, this.

CAR. Well, I'll mark this fellow for Sogliardo's use presently.

PUNT. Or rather, Sogliardo, for his use.

CAR. Faith, either of them will serve, they are both good properties: I'll design the other a place too, that we may see him.

PUNT. No better place than the Mitre, that we may be spectators with you, Carlo. Soft, behold who enters here: ENTER SOGLIARDO. Signior Sogliardo! save you.

SOG. Save you, good sir Puntarvolo; your dog's in health, sir, I see: How now, Carlo?

CAR. We have ta'en simple pains, to choose you out followers here. [SHOWS HIM THE BILLS.

PUNT. Come hither, signior.

CLOVE. Monsieur Orange, yon gallants observe us; prithee let's talk fustian a little, and gull them; make them believe we are great scholars.

ORANGE. O lord, sir!

CLOVE. Nay, prithee let us, believe me,—you have an excellent habit in discourse.

ORANGE. It pleases you to say so, sir.

CLOVE. By this church, you have, la; nay, come, begin—Aristotle, in his daemonologia, approves Scaliger for the best navigator in his time; and in his hypercritics, he reports him to be Heautontimorumenos:—you understand the Greek, sir?

ORANGE. O, good sir!

MACI. For society's sake he does. O, here be a couple of fine tame parrots!

CLOVE. Now, sir, whereas the ingenuity of the time and the soul's synderisis are but embrions in nature, added to the panch of

98

Esquiline, and the inter-vallum of the zodiac, besides the ecliptic line
being optic, and not mental, but by the contemplative and theoric
part thereof, doth demonstrate to us the vegetable circumference,
and the ventosity of the tropics, and whereas our intellectual, or
mincing capreal (according to the metaphysicks) as you may read in
Plato's Histriomastix—You conceive me sir?

ORANGE. O lord, sir!

CLOVE. Then coming to the pretty animal, as reason long since is
fled to animals, you know, or indeed for the more modelising,
or enamelling, or rather diamondising of your subject, you shall
perceive the hypothesis, or galaxia, (whereof the meteors long since
had their initial inceptions and notions,) to be merely Pythagorical,
mathematical, and aristocratical—For, look you, sir, there is ever a
kind of concinnity and species—Let us turn to our former discourse,
for they mark us not.

FAST. Mass, yonder's the knight Puntarvolo.

DELI. And my cousin Sogliardo, methinks.

MACI. Ay, and his familiar that haunts him, the devil with the shining
face.

DELI. Let 'em alone, observe 'em not. [SOGLIARDO, PUNTARVOLO,
AND CARLO, WALK TOGETHER.

SOG. Nay, I will have him, I am resolute for that. By this parchment,
gentlemen, I have been so toiled among the harrots yonder, you will
not believe! they do speak in the strangest language, and give a man
the hardest terms for his money, that ever you knew.

CAR. But have you arms, have you arms?

SOG. I'faith, I thank them; I can write myself gentleman now; here's my
patent, it cost me thirty pound, by this breath.

PUNT. A very fair coat, well charged, and full of armory.

SOG. Nay, it has as much variety of colours in it, as you have seen a coat
have; how like you the crest, sir?

PUNT. I understand it not well, what is't?

SOG. Marry, sir, it is your boar without a head, rampant. A boar without a head, that's very rare!

CAR. Ay, and rampant too! troth, I commend the herald's wit, he has decyphered him well: a swine without a head, without brain, wit, anything indeed, ramping to gentility. You can blazon the rest, signior, can you not?

SOG. O, ay, I have it in writing here of purpose; it cost me two shilling the tricking.

CAR. Let's hear, let's hear.

PUNT. It is the most vile, foolish, absurd, palpable, and ridiculous escutcheon that ever this eye survised.—Save you, good monsieur Fastidious.

    [THEY SALUTE AS THEY MEET IN THE WALK.

COR. Silence, good knight; on, on.

SOG. [READS.] "Gyrony of eight pieces; azure and gules; between three plates, a chevron engrailed checquy, or, vert, and ermins; on a chief argent, between two ann'lets sable, a boar's head, proper."

CAR. How's that! on a chief argent?

SOG. [READS.] "On a chief argent, a boar's head proper, between two ann'lets sable."

CAR. 'Slud, it's a hog's cheek and puddings in a pewter field, this. [HERE THEY SHIFT. FASTIDIOUS MIXES WITH PUNTARVOLO; CARLO AND SOGLIARDO; DELIRO AND MACILENTE; CLOVE AND ORANGE; FOUR COUPLE.

SOG. How like you them, signior?

PUNT. Let the word be, 'Not without mustard': your crest is very rare, sir.

CAR. A frying-pan to the crest, had had no fellow.

FAST. Intreat your poor friend to walk off a little, signior, I will salute the knight.

CAR. Come, lap it up, lap it up.

FAST. You are right well encounter'd, sir; how does your fair dog?

100

PUNT. In reasonable state, sir; what citizen is that you were consorted
    with? A merchant of any worth?
FAST. 'Tis signior Deliro, sir.
PUNT. Is it he?—Save you, sir!   [THEY SALUTE.
DELI. Good sir Puntarvolo!
MACI. O what copy of fool would this place minister, to one endued
    with patience to observe it!
CAR. Nay, look you, sir, now you are a gentleman, you must carry a more
    exalted presence, change your mood and habit to a more austere
    form; be exceeding proud, stand upon your gentility, and scorn every
    man; speak nothing humbly, never discourse under a nobleman,
    though you never saw him but riding to the star-chamber, it's all
    one. Love no man: trust no man: speak ill of no man to his face;
    nor well of any man behind his back. Salute fairly on the front, and
    wish them hanged upon the turn. Spread yourself upon his bosom
    publicly, whose heart you would eat in private. These be principles,
    think on them; I'll come to you again presently.
            [EXIT.
PUNT. [TO HIS SERVANT.] Sirrah, keep close; yet not so close: thy
    breath will thaw my ruff.
SOG. O, good cousin, I am a little busy, how does my niece? I am to walk
    with a knight, here.
    ENTER FUNGOSO WITH HIS TAILOR. FUNG. O, he is here;
    look you, sir, that's the gentleman.
TAI. What, he in the blush-coloured satin?
FUNG. Ay, he, sir; though his suit blush, he blushes not, look you, that's
    the suit, sir: I would have mine such a suit without difference, such
    stuff, such a wing, such a sleeve, such a skirt, belly and all; therefore,
    pray you observe it. Have you a pair of tables?
FAST. Why, do you see, sir, they say I am fantastical; why, true, I know
    it, and I pursue my humour still, in contempt of this censorious
    age. 'Slight, an a man should do nothing but what a sort of stale

judgments about him this town will approve in him, he were a sweet ass: I'd beg him, i'faith. I ne'er knew any more find fault with a fashion, than they that knew not how to put themselves into it. For mine own part, so I please mine own appetite, I am careless what the fusty world speaks of me. Puh!

FUNG. Do you mark, how it hangs at the knee there?

TAI. I warrant you, sir.

FUNG. For God's sake do, not all; do you see the collar, sir?

TAI. Fear nothing, it shall not differ in a stitch, sir.

FUNG. Pray heaven it do not! you'll make these linings serve, and help me to a chapman for the outside, will you?

TAI. I'll do my best, sir: you'll put it off presently.

FUNG. Ay, go with me to my chamber you shall have it—but make haste of it, for the love of a customer; for I'll sit in my old suit, or else lie a bed, and read the 'Arcadia' till you have done.

[EXIT WITH HIS TAILOR.

RE-ENTER CARLO. CAR. O, if ever you were struck with a jest, gallants, now, now, now, I do usher the most strange piece of military profession that ever was discovered in 'Insula Paulina'.

FAST. Where? where?

PUNT. What is he for a creature?

CAR. A pimp, a pimp, that I have observed yonder, the rarest superficies of a humour; he comes every morning to empty his lungs in Paul's here; and offers up some five or six hecatombs of faces and sighs, and away again. Here he comes; nay, walk, walk, be not seen to note him, and we shall have excellent sport.

ENTER SHIFT; AND WALKS BY, USING ACTION TO HIS RAPIER. PUNT. 'Slid, he vented a sigh e'en now, I thought he would have blown up the church.

CAR. O, you shall have him give a number of those false fires ere he depart.

102

FAST. See, now he is expostulating with his rapier: look, look!

CAR. Did you ever in your days observe better passion over a hilt?

PUNT. Except it were in the person of a cutlet's boy, or that the fellow were nothing but vapour, I should think it impossible.

CAR. See again, he claps his sword o' the head, as who should say, well, go to.

FAST. O violence! I wonder the blade can contain itself, being so provoked.

CAR. "With that the moody squire thumpt his breast, And rear'd his eyen to heaven for revenge."

SOG. Troth, an you be good gentlemen, let's make them friends, and take up the matter between his rapier and him.

CAR. Nay, if you intend that, you must lay down the matter; for this rapier, it seems, is in the nature of a hanger-on, and the good gentleman would happily be rid of him.

FAST. By my faith, and 'tis to be suspected; I'll ask him.

MACI. O, here's rich stuff! for life's sake, let us go: A man would wish himself a senseless pillar, Rather than view these monstrous prodigies: "Nil habet infelix paupertas durius in se, Quam quod ridiculos homines facit—"

[EXIT WITH DELIRO.

FAST. Signior.

SHIFT. At your service.

FAST. Will you sell your rapier?

CAR. He is turn'd wild upon the question; he looks as he had seen a serjeant.

SHIFT. Sell my rapier! now fate bless me!

PUNT. Amen.

SHIFT. You ask'd me if I would sell my rapier, sir?

FAST. I did indeed.

SHIFT. Now, lord have mercy upon me!

PUNT. Amen, I say still.

103

SHIFT. 'Slid, sir, what should you behold in my face, sir, that should move you, as they say, sir, to ask me, sir, if I would sell my rapier?

FAST. Nay, let me pray you sir, be not moved: I protest, I would rather have been silent, than any way offensive, had I known your nature.

SHIFT. Sell my rapier? 'ods lid!—Nay, sir, for mine own part, as I am a man that has serv'd in causes, or so, so I am not apt to injure any gentleman in the degree of falling foul, but—sell my rapier! I will tell you, sir, I have served with this foolish rapier, where some of us dare not appear in haste; I name no man; but let that pass. Sell my rapier!—death to my lungs! This rapier, sir, has travell'd by my side, sir, the best part of France, and the Low Country: I have seen Flushing, Brill, and the Hague, with this rapier, sir, in my Lord of Leicester's time; and by God's will, he that should offer to disrapier me now, I would—Look you, sir, you presume to be a gentleman of sort, and so likewise your friends here; if you have any disposition to travel for the sight of service, or so, one, two, or all of you, I can lend you letters to divers officers and commanders in the Low Countries, that shall for my cause do you all the good offices, that shall pertain or belong to gentleman of your—[LOWERING HIS VOICE.] Please you to shew the bounty of your mind, sir, to impart some ten groats, or half a crown to our use, till our ability be of growth to return it, and we shall think oneself—'Sblood! sell my rapier!

SOG. I pray you, what said he, signior? he's a proper man.

FAST. Marry, he tells me, if I please to shew the bounty of my mind, to impart some ten groats to his use, or so—

PUNT. Break his head, and give it him.

CAR. I thought he had been playing o' the Jew's trump, I.

SHIFT. My rapier! no, sir; my rapier is my guard, my defence, my revenue, my honour;—if you cannot impart, be secret, I beseech you—and I will maintain it, where there is a grain of dust, or a drop of water. [SIGHS.] Hard is the choice when the valiant must eat their arms, or clem. Sell my rapier! no, my dear, I will not be divorced from thee, yet; I have ever found thee true as steel, and—You cannot impart, sir?—Save you, gentlemen;—nevertheless, if you have a fancy to it, sir—

FAST. Prithee away: Is signior Deliro departed?

CAR. Have you seen a pimp outface his own wants better?

SOG. I commend him that can dissemble them so well.

PUNT. True, and having no better a cloak for it than he has neither.

FAST. Od's precious, what mischievous luck is this! adieu, gentlemen.

PUNT. Whither in such haste, monsieur Fastidious?

FAST. After my merchant, signior Deliro, sir.

          [EXIT.

CAR. O hinder him not, he may hap lose his title; a good flounder, i'faith.

          [ORANGE AND CLOVE CALL SHIFT ASIDE.

CAR. How! signior Whiffe?

ORANGE. What was the difference between that gallant that's gone and you, sir?

SHIFT. No difference; he would have given me five pound for my rapier, and I refused it; that's all.

CLOVE. O, was it no otherwise? we thought you had been upon some terms.

SHIFT. No other than you saw, sir.

CLOVE. Adieu, good master Apple-John.

          [EXIT WITH ORANGE.

CAR. How! Whiffe, and Apple-John too? Heart, what will you say if this be the appendix or label to both you indentures?

PUNT. It may be.

CAR. Resolve us of it, Janus, thou that look'st every way; or thou, Hercules, that has travelled all countries.

PUNT. Nay, Carlo, spend not time in invocations now, 'tis late.

CAR. Signior, here's a gentleman desirous of your name, sir.

SHIFT. Sir, my name is cavalier Shift: I am known sufficiently in this walk, sir.

CAR. Shift! I heard your name varied even now, as I take it.

SHIFT. True, sir, it pleases the world, as I am her excellent tobacconist, to give me the style of signior Whiffe; as I am a poor esquire about the town here, they call me master Apple-John. Variety of good names does well, sir.

CAR. Ay, and good parts, to make those good names; out of which I imagine yon bills to be yours.

SHIFT. Sir, if I should deny the manuscripts, I were worthy to be banish'd the middle aisle for ever.

CAR. I take your word, sir: this gentleman has subscribed to them, and is most desirous to become your pupil. Marry, you must use expedition. Signior Insulso Sogliardo, this is the professor.

SOG. In good time, sir: nay, good sir, house your head; do you profess these sleights in tobacco?

SHIFT. I do more than profess, sir, and, if you please to be a practitioner, I will undertake in one fortnight to bring you, that you shall take it plausibly in any ordinary, theatre, or the Tilt-yard, if need be, in the most popular assembly that is.

PUNT. But you cannot bring him to the whiffe so soon?

SHIFT. Yes, as soon, sir; he shall receive the first, second, and third whiffe, if it please him, and, upon the receipt, take his horse, drink his three cups of canary, and expose one at Hounslow, a second at Stains, and a third at Bagshot.

CAR. Baw-waw!

SOG. You will not serve me, sir, will you? I'll give you more than countenance.

SHIFT. Pardon me, sir, I do scorn to serve any man.

CAR. Who! he serve? 'sblood, he keeps high men, and low men, he! he has a fair living at Fullam.

SHIFT. But in the nature of a fellow, I'll be your follower, if you please.

SOG. Sir, you shall stay, and dine with me, and if we can agree, we'll not part in haste: I am very bountiful to men of quality. Where shall we go, signior?

PUNT. Your Mitre is your best house.

SHIFT. I can make this dog take as many whiffes as I list, and he shall retain, or effume them, at my pleasure.

PUNT. By your patience, follow me, fellows.

SOG. Sir Puntarvolo!

PUNT. Pardon me, my dog shall not eat in his company for a million.

[EXIT WITH HIS SERVANTS.

CAR. Nay, be not you amazed, signior Whiffe, whatever that stiff-necked gentleman says.

SOG. No, for you do not know the humour of the dog, as we do: Where shall we dine, Carlo? I would fain go to one of these ordinaries, now I am a gentleman.

CAR. So you may; were you never at any yet?

SOG. No, faith; but they say there resorts your most choice gallants.

CAR. True, and the fashion is, when any stranger comes in amongst 'em, they all stand up and stare at him, as he were some unknown beast, brought out of Africk; but that will be helped with a good adventurous face. You must be impudent enough, sit down, and use no respect: when anything's propounded above your capacity smile at it, make two or three faces, and 'tis excellent; they'll think you have travell'd; though you argue, a whole day, in silence thus, and discourse in nothing but laughter, 'twill pass. Only, now and then, give fire, discharge a good full oath, and offer a great wager; 'twill be admirable.

SOG. I warrant you, I am resolute; come, good signior, there's a poor French crown for your ordinary.

SHIFT. It comes well, for I had not so much as the least portcullis of coin before.

MIT. I travail with another objection, signior, which I fear will be enforced against the author, ere I can be deliver'd of it.

COR. What's that sir?

MIT. That the argument of his comedy might have been of some other nature, as of a duke to be in love with a countess, and that countess to be in love with the duke's son, and the son to love the lady's waiting maid; some such cross wooing, with a clown to their servingman, better than to be thus near, and familiarly allied to the time.

COR. You say well, but I would fain hear one of these autumn-judgments define once, "Quid sit comoedia?" if he cannot, let him content himself with Cicero's definition, till he have strength to propose to himself a better, who would have a comedy to be 'imitatio vitae, speculum consuetudinis, imago veritatis'; a thing throughout pleasant and ridiculous, and accommodated to the correction of manners: if the maker have fail'd in any particle of this, they may worthily tax him; but if not, why—be you, that are for them, silent, as I will be for him; and give way to the actors.

SCENE II.—THE COUNTRY.

ENTER SORDIDO, WITH A HALTER ABOUT HIS NECK.

SORD. Nay, God's precious, if the weather and season be so respectless, that beggars shall live as well as their betters; and that my hunger and thirst for riches shall not make them hunger and thirst with poverty; that my sleep shall be broken, and their hearts not broken; that my coffers shall be full, and yet care; their's empty, and yet merry;—'tis time that a cross should bear flesh and blood, since flesh and blood cannot bear this cross.

MIT. What, will he hang himself?

COR. Faith, ay; it seems his prognostication has not kept touch with him, and that makes him despair.

MIT. Beshrew me, he will be 'out of his humour' then indeed.

SORD. Tut, these star-monger knaves, who would trust them? One says dark and rainy, when 'tis as clear as chrystal; another says, tempestuous blasts and storms, and 'twas as calm as a milk-bowl; here be sweet rascals for a man to credit his whole fortunes with! You sky-staring coxcombs you, you fat-brains, out upon you; you are good for nothing but to sweat night-caps, and make rug-gowns dear! you learned men, and have not a legion of devils 'a votre service! a votre service!' by heaven, I think I shall die a better scholar than they: but soft—ENTER A HIND, WITH A LETTER. How now, sirrah?

HIND. Here's a letter come from your son, sir.

SORD. From my son, sir! what would my son, sir? some good news, no doubt. [READS. "Sweet and dear father, desiring you first to send me your blessing, which is more worth to me than gold or silver, I desire you likewise to be advertised, that this Shrove-tide, contrary to custom, we use always to have revels; which is indeed dancing, and makes an excellent shew in truth; especially if we gentlemen be well attired, which our seniors note, and think the better of our fathers, the better we are maintained, and that they shall know if they come up, and have anything to do in the law; therefore, good father, these are, for your own sake as well as mine, to re-desire you, that you let me not want that which is fit for the setting up of our name, in the honourable volume of gentility, that I may say to our calumniators, with Tully, 'Ego sum ortus domus meae, tu occasus tuae.' And thus, not doubting of your fatherly benevolence, I humbly ask your blessing, and pray God to bless you. Yours, if his own," [FUNGOSO.] How's this! "Yours, if his own!" Is he not my son, except he be his own son? belike this is some new kind of subscription the gallants use. Well! wherefore dost thou stay, knave? away; go.

[EXIT HIND.] Here's a letter, indeed! revels? and benevolence? is this a weather to send benevolence? or is this a season to revel in? 'Slid, the devil and all takes part to vex me, I think! this letter would never have come now else, now, now, when the sun shines, and the air thus clear. Soul! If this hold, se shall shortly have an excellent crop of corn spring out of the high ways: the streets and houses of the town will be hid with the rankness of the fruits, that grow there in spite of good husbandry. Go to, I'll prevent the sight of it, come as quickly as it can, I will prevent the sight of it. I have this remedy, heaven. [CLAMBERS UP, AND SUSPENDS THE HALTER TO A TREE.] Stay; I'll try the pain thus a little. O, nothing, nothing. Well now! shall my son gain a benevolence by my death? or anybody be the better for my gold, or so forth? no; alive I kept it from them, and dead, my ghost shall walk about it, and preserve it. My son and daughter shall starve ere they touch it; I have hid it as deep as hell from the sight of heaven, and to it I go now. [FLINGS HIMSELF OFF.

ENTER FIVE OR SIX RUSTICS, ONE AFTER ANOTHER.

1 RUST. Ah me, what pitiful sight is this! help, help, help!

2 RUST. How now! what's the matter?

1 RUST. O, here's a man has hang'd himself, help to get him again.

2 RUST. Hang'd himself! 'Slid, carry him afore a justice, 'tis chance-medley, o' my word.

3 RUST. How now, what's here to do?

4 RUST. How comes this?

2 RUST. One has executed himself, contrary to order of law, and by my consent he shall answer it. [THEY CUT HIM DOWN.

5 RUST. Would he were in case to answer it!

1 RUST. Stand by, he recovers, give him breath.

SORD. Oh!

5 RUST. Mass, 'twas well you went the footway, neighbour.

1 RUST. Ay, an I had not cut the halter—

SORD. How! cut the halter! ah me, I am undone, I am undone!

2 RUST. Marry, if you had not been undone, you had been hang'd. I can tell you.

SORD. You thread-bare, horse-bread-eating rascals, if you would needs have been meddling, could you not have untied it, but you must cut it; and in the midst too! ah me!

1 RUST. Out on me, 'tis the caterpillar Sordido! how curst are the poor, that the viper was blest with this good fortune!

2 RUST. Nay, how accurst art thou, that art cause to the curse of the poor?

3 RUST. Ay, and to save so wretched a caitiff?

4 RUST. Curst be thy fingers that loos'd him!

2 RUST. Some desperate fury possess thee, that thou may'st hang thyself too!

5 RUST. Never may'st thou be saved, that saved so damn'd a monster!

SORD. What curses breathe these men! how have my deeds
 Made my looks differ from another man's,
 That they should thus detest and loath my life!
 Out on my wretched humour! it is that
 Makes me thus monstrous in true humane eyes.
 Pardon me, gentle friends, I'll make fair 'mends
 For my foul errors past, and twenty-fold
 Restore to all men, what with wrong I robb'd them:
 My barns and garners shall stand open still
 To all the poor that come, and my best grain
 Be made alms-bread, to feed half-famish'd mouths.
 Though hitherto amongst you I have lived,
 Like an unsavoury muck-hill to myself,
 Yet now my gather'd heaps being spread abroad,
 Shall turn to better and more fruitful uses.
 Bless then this man, curse him no more for the saving
 My life and soul together. O how deeply

The bitter curses of the poor do pierce!
I am by wonder changed; come in with me
And witness my repentance: now I prove,
No life is blest, that is not graced with love.

[EXIT.

2 RUST. O miracle! see when a man has grace!

3 RUST. Had it not been pity so good a man should have been cast away?

2 RUST. Well, I'll get our clerk put his conversion in the 'Acts and Monuments'.

4 RUST. Do, for I warrant him he's a martyr.

2 RUST. O God, how he wept, if you mark'd it! did you see how the tears trill'd?

5 RUST. Yes, believe me, like master vicar's bowls upon the green, for all the world.

3 RUST. O neighbour, God's blessing o' your heart, neighbour, 'twas a good grateful deed. [EXEUNT.

COR. How now, Mitis! what's that you consider so seriously?

MIT. Troth, that which doth essentially please me, the warping condition of this green and soggy multitude; but in good faith, signior, your author hath largely outstript my expectation in this scene, I will liberally confess it. For when I saw Sordido so desperately intended, I thought I had had a hand of him, then.

COR. What! you supposed he should have hung himself indeed?

MIT. I did, and had framed my objection to it ready, which may yet be very fitly urged, and with some necessity; for though his purposed violence lost the effect, and extended not to death, yet the intent and horror of the object was more than the nature of a comedy will in any sort admit.

COR. Ay! what think you of Plautus, in his comedy called 'Cistellaria'? there, where he brings in Alcesimarchus with a drum sword ready

112

to kill himself, and as he is e'en fixing his breast upon it, to be restrained from his resolved outrage, by Silenium and the bawd? Is not his authority of power to give our scene approbation?

MIT. Sir, I have this only evasion left me, to say, I think it be so indeed; your memory is happier than mine: but I wonder, what engine he will use to bring the rest out of their humours!

COR. That will appear anon, never pre-occupy your imagination withal. Let your mind keep company with the scene still, which now removes itself from the country to the court. Here comes Macilente, and signior Brisk freshly suited; lose not yourself, for now the epitasis, or busy part of our subject, is an act.

SCENE III.—AN APARTMENT AT THE COURT

ENTER MACILENTE, FASTIDIOUS, BOTH IN A NEW SUIT, AND CINEDO, WITH TOBACCO.

FAST. Well, now signior Macilente, you are not only welcome to the court, but also to my mistress's withdrawing chamber—Boy, get me some tobacco. I'll but go in, and shew I am here, and come to you presently, sir.

[EXIT.

MACI. What's that he said? by heaven, I mark'd him not:
My thoughts and I were of another world.
I was admiring mine own outside here,
To think what privilege and palm it bears
Here, in the court! be a man ne'er so vile,
In wit, in judgment, manners, or what else;
If he can purchase but a silken cover,
He shall not only pass, but pass regarded:
Whereas, let him be poor, and meanly clad,

113

Though ne'er so richly parted, you shall have
A fellow that knows nothing but his beef,
Or how to rince his clammy guts in beer,
Will take him by the shoulders, or the throat,
And kick him down the stairs. Such is the state
Of virtue in bad clothes!—ha, ha, ha, ha!
That raiment should be in such high request!
How long should I be, ere I should put off
To the lord chancellor's tomb, or the shrives' poste?
By heav'n, I think, a thousand, thousand year.
His gravity, his wisdom, and his faith
To my dread sovereign, graces that survive him,
These I could well endure to reverence,
But not his tomb; no more than I'd commend
The chapel organ for the gilt without,
Or this base-viol, for the varnish'd face.
RE-ENTER FASTIDIOUS. FAST. I fear I have made you stay somewhat long, sir; but is my tobacco ready, boy?

CIN. Ay, sir.

FAST. Give me; my mistress is upon coming, you shall see her presently, sir. [PUFFS.] You'll say you never accosted a more piercing wit.— This tobacco is not dried, boy, or else the pipe is defective.—Oh, your wits of Italy are nothing comparable to her: her brain's a very quiver of jests, and she does dart them abroad with that sweet, loose, and judicial aim, that you would—here she comes, sir. [SAVIOLINA LOOKS IN, AND DRAWS BACK AGAIN.

MACI. 'Twas time, his invention had been bogged else.

SAV. [WITHIN.] Give me my fan there.

MACI. How now, monsieur Brisk?

FAST. A kind of affectionate reverence strikes me with a cold shivering, methinks.

MACI. I like such tempers well, as stand before their mistresses with fear and trembling; and before their Maker, like impudent mountains!

FAST. By this hand, I'd spend twenty pound my vaulting horse stood here now, she might see do but one trick.

MACI. Why, does she love activity?

CIN. Or, if you had but your long stockings on, to be dancing a galliard as she comes by.

FAST. Ay, either. O, these stirring humours make ladies mad with desire; she comes. My good genius embolden me: boy, the pipe quickly. ENTER SAVIOLINA. MACI. What! will he give her music?

FAST. A second good morrow to my fair mistress.

SAV. Fair servant, I'll thank you a day hence, when the date of your salutation comes forth.

FAST. How like you that answer? is't not admirable?

MACI. I were a simple courtier, if I could not admire trifles, sir.

FAST. [TALKS AND TAKES TOBACCO BETWEEN THE BREAKS.] Troth, sweet lady, I shall [PUFFS]—be prepared to give you thanks for those thanks, and—study more officious, and obsequious regards—to your fair beauties.—Mend the pipe, boy.

MACI. I never knew tobacco taken as a parenthesis before.

FAST. 'Fore God, sweet lady, believe it, I do honour the meanest rush in this chamber for your love.

SAV. Ay, you need not tell me that, sir; I do think you do prize a rush before my love.

MACI. Is this the wonder of nations!

FAST. O, by this air, pardon me, I said 'for' your love, by this light: but it is the accustomed sharpness of your ingenuity, sweet mistress, to [TAKES DOWN THE VIOL, AND PLAYS]—mass, your viol's new strung, methinks.

MACI. Ingenuity! I see his ignorance will not suffer him to slander her, which he had done notably, if he had said wit for ingenuity, as he meant it.

FAST. By the soul of music, lady—HUM, HUM.

SAV. Would we might hear it once.

FAST. I do more adore and admire your—HUM, HUM—predominant perfections, than—HUM, HUM—ever I shall have power and faculty to express—HUM.

SAV. Upon the viol de gambo, you mean?

FAST. It's miserably out of tune, by this hand.

SAV. Nay, rather by the fingers.

MACI. It makes good harmony with her wit.

FAST. Sweet lady, tune it. [SAVIOLINA TUNES THE VIOL.]—Boy, some tobacco.

MACI. Tobacco again! he does court his mistress with very exceeding good changes.

FAST. Signior Macilente, you take none, sir?

MACI. No, unless I had a mistress, signior, it were a great indecorum for me to take tobacco.

FAST. How like you her wit? [TALKS AND TAKES TOBACCO BETWEEN AGAIN.

MACI. Her ingenuity is excellent, sir.

FAST. You see the subject of her sweet fingers there—Oh, she tickles it so, that—She makes it laugh most divinely;—I'll tell you a good jest now, and yourself shall say it's a good one: I have wished myself to be that instrument, I think, a thousand times, and not so few, by heaven!—

MACI. Not unlike, sir; but how? to be cased up and hung by on the wall?

FAST. O, no, sir, to be in use, I assure you; as your judicious eyes may testify.—

SAV. Here, servant, if you will play, come.

FAST. Instantly, sweet lady.—In good faith, here's most divine tobacco!

SAV. Nay, I cannot stay to dance after your pipe.

116

FAST. Good! Nay, dear lady, stay; by this sweet smoke, I think your wit be all fire.—

MACI. And he's the salamander belongs to it.

SAV. Is your tobacco perfumed, servant, that you swear by the sweet smoke?

FAST. Still more excellent! Before heaven, and these bright lights, I think—you are made of ingenuity, I—

MACI. True, as your discourse is. O abominable!

FAST. Will your ladyship take any?

SAV. O peace, I pray you; I love not the breath of a woodcock's head.

FAST. Meaning my head, lady?

SAV. Not altogether so, sir; but, as it were fatal to their follies that think to grace themselves with taking tobacco, when they want better entertainment, you see your pipe bears the true form of a woodcock's head.

FAST. O admirable simile!

AV. 'Tis best leaving of you in admiration, sir.
                    [EXIT.

MACI. Are these the admired lady-wits, that having so good a plain song, can run no better division upon it? All her jests are of the stamp March was fifteen years ago. Is this the comet, monsieur Fastidious, that your gallants wonder at so?

FAST. Heart of a gentleman, to neglect me afore the presence thus! Sweet sir, I beseech you be silent in my disgrace. By the muses, I was never in so vile a humour in my life, and her wit was at the flood too! Report it not for a million, good sir: let me be so far endeared to your love. [EXEUNT.

MIT. What follows next, signior Cordatus? this gallant's humour is almost spent; methinks it ebbs apace, with this contrary breath of his mistress.

COR. O, but it will flow again for all this, till there come a general drought of humour among our actors, and then I fear not but his will fall as low as any. See who presents himself here!

MIT. What, in the old case?

COR. Ay, faith, which makes it the more pitiful; you understand where the scene is?

ACT IV

SCENE I.—A ROOM IN DELIRO'S HOUSE.

ENTER FUNGOSO, FALLACE FOLLOWING HIM.

FAL. Why are you so melancholy, brother?

FUNG. I am not melancholy, I thank you, sister.

FAL. Why are you not merry then? there are but two of us in all the world, and if we should not be comforts one to another, God help us!

FUNG. Faith, I cannot tell, sister; but if a man had any true melancholy in him, it would make him melancholy to see his yeomanly father cut his neighbours' throats, to make his son a gentleman; and yet, when he has cut them, he will see his son's throat cut too, ere he make him a true gentleman indeed, before death cut his own throat. I must be the first head of our house, and yet he will not give me the head till I be made so. Is any man termed a gentleman, that is not always in the fashion? I would know but that.

FAL. If you be melancholy for that, brother, I think I have as much cause to be melancholy as any one: for I'll be sworn, I live as little in the fashion as any woman in London. By the faith of a gentlewoman, beast that I am to say it! I have not one friend in the world besides my husband. When saw you master Fastidious Brisk, brother?

FUNG. But a while since, sister, I think: I know not well in truth. By this hand I could fight with all my heart, methinks.

FAL. Nay, good brother, be not resolute.

FUNG. I sent him a letter, and he writes me no answer neither.

FAL. Oh, sweet Fastidious Brisk! O fine courtier! thou are he makest me sigh, and say, how blessed is that woman that hath a courtier to her husband, and how miserable a dame she is, that hath neither husband, nor friend in the court! O sweet Fastidious! O fine courtier! How comely he bows him in his court'sy! how full he hits a woman between the lips when he kisses! how upright he sits at the table! how daintily he carves! how sweetly he talks, and tells news of this lord and of that lady! how cleanly he wipes his spoon at every spoonful of any whitemeat he eats! and what a neat case of pick-tooths he carries about him still! O sweet Fastidious! O fine courtier!

ENTER DELIRO AT A DISTANCE, WITH MUSICIANS. DELI. See, yonder she is, gentlemen. Now, as ever you'll bear the name of musicians, touch your instruments sweetly; she has a delicate ear, I tell you: play not a false note, I beseech you.

MUSI. Fear not, signior Deliro.

DELI. O, begin, begin, some sprightly thing: lord, how my imagination labours with the success of it! [THEY STRIKE UP A LIVELY TUNE.] Well said, good i'faith! Heaven grant it please her. I'll not be seen, for then she'll be sure to dislike it.

FAL. Hey—da! this is excellent! I'll lay my life this is my husband's dotage. I thought so; nay, never play bo-peep with me; I know you do nothing but study how to anger me, sir.

DELI. [COMING FORWARD.] Anger thee, sweet wife! why, didst thou not send for musicians at supper last night thyself?

FAL. To supper, sir! now, come up to supper, I beseech you: as though there were no difference between supper-time, when folks should be merry, and this time when they should be melancholy. I would never take upon me to take a wife, if I had no more judgment to please her.

DELI. Be pleased, sweet wife, and they shall have done; and would to fate my life were done, if I can never please thee! [EXEUNT MUSICIANS.

ENTER MACILENTE. MACI. Save you lady; where is master Deliro?

DELI. Here, master Macilente: you are welcome from court, sir; no doubt you have been graced exceedingly of master Brisk's mistress, and the rest of the ladies for his sake.

MACI. Alas, the poor fantastic! he's scarce known
    To any lady there; and those that know him,
    Know him the simplest man of all they know:
    Deride, and play upon his amorous humours,
    Though he but apishly doth imitate
    The gallant'st courtiers, kissing ladies' pumps,
    Holding the cloth for them, praising their wits,
    And servilely observing every one
    May do them pleasure: fearful to be seen
    With any man, though he be ne'er so worthy,
    That's not in grace with some that are the greatest.
    Thus courtiers do, and these he counterfeits,
    But sets no such a sightly carriage
    Upon their vanities, as they themselves;
    And therefore they despise him: for indeed
    He's like the zany to a tumbler,
    That tries tricks after him, to make men laugh.

FAL. Here's an unthankful spiteful wretch! the good gentleman vouchsafed to make him his companion, because my husband put him into a few rags, and now see how the unrude rascal backbites him! [ASIDE.

DELI. Is he no more graced amongst them then, say you?

MACI. Faith, like a pawn at chess: fills up a room, that's all.

120

FAL. O monster of men! can the earth bear such an envious caitiff?
    [ASIDE.
DELI. Well, I repent me I ever credited him so much: but now I see what
    he is, and that his masking vizor is off, I'll forbear him no longer.
    All his lands are mortgaged to me, and forfeited; besides, I have
    bonds of his in my hand, for the receipt of now fifty pounds now
    a hundred, now two hundred; still, as he has had a fan but wagged
    at him, he would be in a new suit. Well, I'll salute him by a serjeant,
    the next time I see him i'faith, I'll suit him.
MACI. Why, you may soon see him sir, for he is to meet signior Puntarvolo
    at a notary's by the Exchange, presently; where he meant to take up,
    upon return.
FAL. Now, out upon thee, Judas! canst thou not be content to backbite
    thy friend, but thou must betray him! Wilt thou seek the undoing of
    any man? and of such a man too? and will you, sir, get your living
    by the counsel of traitors?
DELI. Dear wife, have patience.
FAL. The house will fall, the ground will open and swallow us: I'll not
    bide here for all the gold and silver in heaven.
    [EXIT WITH FUNGOSO.
DELI. O, good Macilente, let's follow and appease her, or the peace
    of my life is at an end.
    [EXIT.
MACI. Now pease, and not peace, feed that life, whose head hangs so
    heavily over a woman's manger!
    [EXIT.

SCENE II.—ANOTHER ROOM IN THE SAME.
ENTER FALLACE AND FUNGOSO RUNNING; SHE
CLAPS TO THE DOOR.

FAL. Help me, brother! Ods body, an you come here I'll do myself a
    mischief.
                                                            121

DELI. [WITHIN.] Nay, hear me, sweet wife; unless thou wilt have me go, I will not go.

FAL. Tut, you shall never have that vantage of me, to say, you are undone by me. I'll not bid you stay, I. Brother, sweet brother, here's four angels, I'll give you towards your suit: for the love of gentry, and as ever you came of Christian creature, make haste to the water side, (you know where master Fastidious uses to land,) and give him warning of my husband's malicious intent; and tell him of that lean rascal's treachery. O heavens, how my flesh rises at him! Nay, sweet brother, make haste: you may say, I would have writ to him, but that the necessity of the time would not permit. He cannot choose but take it extraordinarily from me: and commend me to him, good brother; say, I sent you.

           [EXIT.

FUNG. Let me see, these four angels, and then forty shillings more I can borrow on my gown in Fetter Lane.—Well, I will go presently, say on my suit, pay as much money as I have, and swear myself into credit with my tailor for the rest.

           [EXIT.

SCENE III.—ANOTHER ROOM IN THE SAME.

ENTER DELIRO AND MACILENTE.

DELI. O, on my soul you wrong her, Macilente. Though she be froward, yet I know she is honest.

MACI. Well, then have I no judgment. Would any woman, but one that were wild in her affections, have broke out into that immodest and violent passion against her husband? or is't possible—

DELI. If you love me, forbear; all the arguments i' the world shall never wrest my heart to believe it. [EXEUNT.

COR. How like you the deciphering of his dotage?

122

MIT. O, strangely: an of the other's envy too, that labours so seriously to set debate betwixt a man and his wife. Stay, here comes the knight adventurer.

COR. Ay, and his scrivener with him.

SCENE IV.—PUNTARVOLO'S LODGINGS.

ENTER PUNTARVOLO, NOTARY, AND SERVANTS WITH THE DOG AND CAT.

PUNT. I wonder monsieur Fastidious comes not! But, notary, if thou please to draw the indentures the while, I will give thee thy instructions.

NOT. With all my heart, sir; and I'll fall in hand with them presently.

PUNT. Well then, first the sum is to be understood.

NOT. [WRITES.] Good, sir.

PUNT. Next, our several appellations, and character of my dog and cat, must be known. Shew him the cat, sirrah.

NOT. So, sir.

PUNT. Then, that the intended bound is the Turk's court in Constantinople; the time limited for our return, a year; and that if either of us miscarry, the whole venture is lost. These are general, conceiv'st thou? or if either of us turn Turk.

NOT. Ay, sir.

PUNT. Now, for particulars: that I may make my travels by sea or land, to my best liking; and that hiring a coach for myself, it shall be lawful for my dog or cat, or both, to ride with me in the said coach.

NOT. Very good, sir.

PUNT. That I may choose to give my dog or cat, fish, for fear of bones; or any other nutriment that, by the judgment of the most authentical physicians where I travel, shall be thought dangerous.

NOT. Well, sir.

PUNT. That, after the receipt of his money, he shall neither, in his own person, nor any other, either by direct or indirect means, as magic, witchcraft, or other such exotic arts, attempt, practise, or complot any thing to the prejudice of me, my dog, or my cat: neither shall I use the help of any such sorceries or enchantments, as unctions to make our skins impenetrable, or to travel invisible by virtue of a powder, or a ring, or to hang any three-forked charm about my dog's neck, secretly conveyed into his collar; (understand you?) but that all be performed sincerely, without fraud or imposture.

NOT. So, sir.

PUNT. That, for testimony of the performance, myself am to bring thence a Turk's mustachio, my dog a Grecian hare's lips, and my cat the train or tail of a Thracian rat.

NOT. [WRITES.] 'Tis done, sir.

PUNT. 'Tis said, sir; not done, sir. But forward; that, upon my return, and landing on the Tower-wharf, with the aforesaid testimony, I am to receive five for one, according to the proportion of the sums put forth.

NOT. Well, sir.

PUNT. Provided, that if before our departure, or setting forth, either myself or these be visited with sickness, or any other casual event, so that the whole course of the adventure be hindered thereby, that then he is to return, and I am to receive the prenominated proportion upon fair and equal terms.

NOT. Very good, sir; is this all?

PUNT. It is all, sir; and dispatch them, good notary.

NOT. As fast as is possible, sir.
                    [EXIT.

ENTER CARLO. PUNT. O Carlo! welcome: saw you monsieur Brisk?

CAR. Not I: did he appoint you to meet here?

PUNT. Ay, and I muse he should be so tardy; he is to take an hundred pounds of me in venture, if he maintain his promise.

CAR. Is his hour past?

PUNT. Not yet, but it comes on apace.

CAR. Tut, be not jealous of him; he will sooner break all the commandments, than his hour; upon my life, in such a case trust him.

PUNT. Methinks, Carlo, you look very smooth, ha!

CAR. Why, I came but now from a hot-house; I must needs look smooth.

PUNT. From a hot-house!

CAR. Ay, do you make a wonder on't? why, it is your only physic. Let a man sweat once a week in a hot-house, and be well rubb'd, and froted, with a good plump juicy wench, and sweet linen, he shall ne'er have the pox.

PUNT. What, the French pox?

CAR. The French pox! out pox: we have them in as good a form as they, man; what?

PUNT. Let me perish, but thou art a salt one! was your new-created gallant there with you, Sogliardo?

CAR. O porpoise! hang him, no: he's a leiger at Horn's ordinary, yonder; his villainous Ganymede and he have been droning a tobacco-pipe there ever since yesterday noon.

PUNT. Who? signior Tripartite, that would give my dog the whiffe?

CAR. Ay, he. They have hired a chamber and all, private, to practise in, for the making of the patoun, the receipt reciprocal, and a number of other mysteries not yet extant. I brought some dozen or twenty gallants this morning to view them, as you'd do a piece of perspective, in at a key-hole; and there we might see Sogliardo sit in a chair, holding his snout up like a sow under an apple-tree, while the other open'd his nostrils with a poking-stick, to give the smoke a more free delivery. They had spit some three or fourscore ounces between 'em, afore we came away.

PUNT. How! spit three or fourscore ounces?

125

CAR. Ay, and preserv'd it in porrengers, as a barber does his blood, when he opens a vein.

PUNT. Out, pagan! how dost thou open the vein of thy friend?

CAR. Friend! is there any such foolish thing in the world, ha? 'slid I never relished it yet.

PUNT. Thy humour is the more dangerous.

CAR. No, not a whit, signior. Tut, a man must keep time in all; I can oil my tongue when I meet him next, and look with a good sleek forehead; 'twill take away all soil of suspicion, and that's enough: what Lynceus can see my heart? Pish, the title of a friend! it's a vain, idle thing, only venerable among fools; you shall not have one that has any opinion of wit affect it.

ENTER DELIRO AND MACILENTE. DELI. Save you, good sir Puntarvolo.

PUNT. Signior Deliro! welcome.

DELI. Pray you, sir, did you see master Fastidious Brisk? I heard he was to meet your worship here.

PUNT. You heard no figment, sir; I do expect him at every pulse of my watch.

DELI. In good time, sir.

CAR. There's a fellow now looks like one of the patricians of Sparta; marry, his wit's after ten i' the hundred: a good bloodhound, a close-mouthed dog, he follows the scent well; marry, he's at fault now, methinks.

PUNT. I should wonder at that creature is free from the danger of thy tongue.

CAR. O, I cannot abide these limbs of satin, or rather Satan indeed, that will walk, like the children of darkness, all day in a melancholy shop, with their pockets full of blanks, ready to swallow up as many poor unthrifts as come within the verge.

PUNT. So! and what hast thou for him that is with him, now?

CAR. O, d—n me! immortality! I'll not meddle with him; the pure element of fire, all spirit, extraction.

PUNT. How, Carlo! ha, what is he, man?

CAR. A scholar, Macilente; do you not know him? a rank, raw-boned anatomy, he walks up and down like a charged musket, no man dares encounter him: that's his rest there.

PUNT. His rest! why, has he a forked head?

CAR. Pardon me, that's to be suspended; you are too quick, too apprehensive.

DELI. Troth, now I think on't, I'll defer it till some other time.

MACI. Not by any means, signior, you shall not lose this opportunity, he will be here presently now.

DELI. Yes, faith, Macilente, 'tis best. For, look you, sir, I shall so exceedingly offend my wife in't, that—

MACI. Your wife! now for shame lose these thoughts, and become the master of your own spirits. Should I, if I had a wife, suffer myself to be thus passionately carried to and fro with the stream of her humour, and neglect my deepest affairs, to serve her affections? 'Slight, I would geld myself first.

DELI. O, but signior, had you such a wife as mine is, you would—

MACI. Such a wife! Now hate me, sir, if ever I discern'd any wonder in your wife yet, with all the speculation I have: I have seen some that have been thought fairer than she, in my time; and I have seen those, have not been altogether so tall, esteem'd properer women; and I have seen less noses grow upon sweeter faces, that have done very well too, in my judgment. But in good faith, signior, for all this, the gentlewoman is a good, pretty, proud, hard-favour'd thing, marry not so peerlessly to be doted upon, I must confess: nay, be not angry.

DELI. Well, sir, however you please to forget yourself, I have not deserv'd to be thus played upon; but henceforth, pray you forbear my house, for I can but faintly endure the savour of his breath, at my table, that shall thus jade me for my courtesies.

MACI. Nay, then, signior, let me tell you, your wife is no proper woman, and by my life, I suspect her honesty, that's more, which you may likewise suspect, if you please, do you see? I'll urge you to nothing against your appetite, but if you please, you may suspect it.

DELI. Good sir.

[EXIT.

MACI. Good, sir! now horn upon horn pursue thee, thou blind, egregious dotard!

CAR. O, you shall hear him speak like envy.—Signior Macilente, you saw monsieur Brisk lately: I heard you were with him at court.

MACI. Ay, Buffone, I was with him.

CAR. And how is he respected there? I know you'll deal ingenuously with us; is he made much of amongst the sweeter sort of gallants?

MACI. Faith, ay; his civet and his casting-glass
    Have helpt him to a place amongst the rest:
    And there, his seniors give him good slight looks,
    After their garb, smile, and salute in French
    With some new compliment.

CAR. What, is this all?

MACI. Why say, that they should shew the frothy fool
    Such grace as they pretend comes from the heart,
    He had a mighty windfall out of doubt!
    Why, all their graces are not to do grace
    To virtue or desert; but to ride both
    With their gilt spurs quite breathless, from themselves.
    'Tis now esteem'd precisianism in wit,
    And a disease in nature, to be kind
    Toward desert, to love or seek good names.
    Who feeds with a good name? who thrives with loving?
    Who can provide feast for his own desires,

With serving others?—ha, ha, ha!

'Tis folly, by our wisest worldlings proved,

If not to gain by love, to be beloved.

CAR. How like you him? is't not a good spiteful slave, ha?

PUNT. Shrewd, shrewd.

CAR. D—n me! I could eat his flesh now; divine sweet villain!

MACI. Nay, prithee leave: What's he there?

CAR. Who? this in the starched beard? it's the dull stiff knight Puntarvolo, man; he's to travel now presently: he has a good knotty wit; marry, he carries little on't out of the land with him.

MACI. How then?

CAR. He puts it forth in venture, as he does his money upon the return of a dog and cat.

MACI. Is this he?

CAR. Ay, this is he; a good tough gentleman: he looks like a shield of brawn at Shrove-tide, out of date, and ready to take his leave; or a dry pole of ling upon Easter-eve, that has furnish'd the table all Lent, as he has done the city this last vacation.

MACI. Come, you'll never leave your stabbing similes: I shall have you aiming at me with 'em by and by; but—

CAR. O, renounce me then! pure, honest, good devil, I love thee above the love of women: I could e'en melt in admiration of thee, now. Ods so, look here, man; Sir Dagonet and his squire!

ENTER SOGLIARDO AND SHIFT. SOG. Save you, my dear gallantos: nay, come, approach, good cavalier: prithee, sweet knight, know this gentleman, he's one that it pleases me to use as my good friend and companion; and therefore do him good offices: I beseech you, gentles, know him, I know him all over.

PUNT. Sir, for signior Sogliardo's sake, let it suffice, I know you.

SOG. Why, as I am a gentleman, I thank you, knight, and it shall suffice. Hark you, sir Puntarvolo, you'd little think it; he's as resolute a piece of flesh as any in the world.

PUNT. Indeed, sir!

SOG. Upon my gentility, sir: Carlo, a word with you; do you see that same fellow, there?

CAR. What, cavalier Shirt?

SOG. O, you know him; cry you mercy: before me, I think him the tallest man living within the walls of Europe.

CAR. The walls of Europe! take heed what you say, signior, Europe's a huge thing within the walls.

SOG. 'Tut, an 'twere as huge again, I'd justify what I speak. 'Slid, he swagger'd even now in a place where we were—I never saw a man do it more resolute.

CAR. Nay, indeed, swaggering is a good argument of resolution. Do you hear this, signior?

MACI. Ay, to my grief. O, that such muddy flags,
    For every drunken flourish should achieve
    The name of manhood, whilst true perfect valour,
    Hating to shew itself, goes by despised!
    Heart! I do know now, in a fair just cause,
    I dare do more than he, a thousand times;
    Why should not they take knowledge of this, ha!
    And give my worth allowance before his?
    Because I cannot swagger.—Now, the pox
    Light on your Pickt-hatch prowess!

SOG. Why, I tell you, sir; he has been the only 'Bid-stand' that ever kept New-market, Salisbury-plain, Hockley i' the Hole, Gadshill, and all the high places of any request: he has had his mares and his geldings, he, have been worth forty, threescore, a hundred pound a horse, would ha' sprung you over the hedge and ditch like your greyhound: he has done five hundred robberies in his time, more or less, I assure you.

PUNT. What, and scaped?

130

SOG. Scaped! i'faith, ay: he has broken the gaol when he has been in irons and irons; and been out and in again; and out, and in; forty times, and not so few, he.

MACI. A fit trumpet, to proclaim such a person.

CAR. But can this be possible?

SHIFT. Pardon me, my dear Orestes; causes have their quiddits, and 'tis ill jesting with bell-ropes.

CAR. How! Pylades and Orestes?

SOG. Ay, he is my Pylades, and I am his Orestes: how like you the conceit?

CAR. O, 'tis an old stale interlude device; no, I'll give you names myself, look you; he shall be your Judas, and you shall be his elder-tree to hang on.

MACI. Nay, rather let him be captain Pod, and this his motion: for he does nothing but shew him.

CAR. Excellent: or thus; you shall be Holden, and he your camel.

SHIFT. You do not mean to ride, gentlemen?

PUNT. Faith, let me end it for you, gallants: you shall be his Countenance, and he your Resolution.

SOG. Troth, that's pretty: how say you, cavalier, shall it be so?

CAR. Ay, ay, most voices.

SHIFT. Faith, I am easily yielding to any good impressions.

SOG. Then give hands, good Resolution.

CAR. Mass, he cannot say, good Countenance, now, properly, to him again.

PUNT. Yes, by an irony.

MACI. O, sir, the countenance of Resolution should, as he is, be altogether grim and unpleasant.

ENTER FASTIDIOUS BRISK. FAST. Good hours make music with your mirth, gentlemen, and keep time to your humours!—How now, Carlo?

PUNT. Monsieur Brisk? many a long look have I extended for you, sir.

FAST. Good faith, I must crave pardon: I was invited this morning, ere I was out of my bed, by a bevy of ladies, to a banquet: whence it was almost one of Hercules's labours for me to come away, but that the respect of my promise did so prevail with me. I know they'll take it very ill, especially one, that gave me this bracelet of her hair but over night, and this pearl another gave me from her forehead, marry she—what! are the writings ready?

PUNT. I will send my man to know. Sirrah, go you to the notary's, and learn if he be ready: leave the dog, sir.

[EXIT SERVANT.

FAST. And how does my rare qualified friend, Sogliardo? Oh, signior Macilente! by these eyes, I saw you not; I had saluted you sooner else, o' my troth. I hope, sir, I may presume upon you, that you will not divulge my late check, or disgrace, indeed, sir.

MACI. You may, sir.

CAR. He knows some notorious jest by this gull, that he hath him so obsequious.

SOG. Monsieur Fastidious, do you see this fellow there? does he not look like a clown? would you think there were any thing in him?

FAST. Any thing in him! beshrew me, ay; the fellow hath a good ingenious face.

SOG. By this element he is as ingenious a tall man as ever swagger'd about London: he, and I, call Countenance and Resolution; but his name is cavalier Shift.

PUNT. Cavalier, you knew signior Clog, that was hang'd for the robbery at Harrow on the hill?

SOG. Knew him, sir! why, 'twas he gave all the directions for the action.

PUNT. How! was it your project, sir?

SHIFT. Pardon me, Countenance, you do me some wrong to make occasions public, which I imparted to you in private.

SOG. God's will! here are none but friends, Resolution.

132

SHIFT. That's all one; things of consequence must have their respects; where, how, and to whom.—Yes, sir, he shewed himself a true Clog in the coherence of that affair, sir; for, if he had managed matters as they were corroborated to him, it had been better for him by a forty or fifty score of pounds, sir; and he himself might have lived, in despight of fates, to have fed on woodcocks, with the rest: but it was his heavy fortune to sink, poor Clog! and therefore talk no more of him.

PUNT. Why, had he more aiders then?

SOG. O lord, sir! ay, there were some present there, that were the Nine Worthies to him, i'faith.

SHIFT. Ay, sir, I can satisfy you at more convenient conference: but, for mine own part, I have now reconciled myself to other courses, and profess a living out of my other qualities.

SOG. Nay, he has left all now, I assure you, and is able to live like a gentleman, by his qualities. By this dog, he has the most rare gift in tobacco that ever you knew.

CAR. He keeps more ado with this monster, than ever Banks did with his horse, or the fellow with the elephant.

MACI. He will hang out his picture shortly, in a cloth, you shall see.

SOG. O, he does manage a quarrel the best that ever you saw, for terms and circumstances.

FAST. Good faith, signior, now you speak of a quarrel, I'll acquaint you with a difference that happened between a gallant and myself; sir Puntarvolo, you know him if I should name him signior Luculento.

PUNT. Luculento! what inauspicious chance interposed itself to your two loves?

FAST. Faith, sir, the same that sundered Agamemnon and great Thetis' son; but let the cause escape, sir: he sent me a challenge, mixt with some few braves, which I restored, and in fine we met. Now, indeed, sir, I must tell you, he did offer at first very desperately, but without

133

judgment: for, look you, sir, I cast myself into this figure; now he comes violently on, and withal advancing his rapier to strike, I thought to have took his arm, for he had left his whole body to my election, and I was sure he could not recover his guard. Sir, I mist my purpose in his arm, rash'd his doublet-sleeve, ran him close by the left cheek, and through his hair. He again lights me here,—I had on a gold cable hatband, then new come up, which I wore about a murey French hat I had,—cuts my hatband, and yet it was massy goldsmith's work, cuts my brims, which by good fortune, being thick embroidered with gold twist and spangles, disappointed the force of the blow: nevertheless, it grazed on my shoulder, takes me away six purls of an Italian cut-work band I wore, cost me three pound in the Exchange but three days before.

PUNT. This was a strange encounter.

FAST. Nay, you shall hear, sir: with this we both fell out, and breath'd. Now, upon the second sign of his assault, I betook me to the former manner of my defence; he, on the other side, abandon'd his body to the same danger as before, and follows me still with blows: but I being loth to take the deadly advantage that lay before me of his left side, made a kind of stramazoun, ran him up to the hilts through the doublet, through the shirt, and yet miss'd the skin. He, making a reverse blow,—falls upon my emboss'd girdle, I had thrown off the hangers a little before—strikes off a skirt of a thick-laced satin doublet I had, lined with four taffatas, cuts off two panes embroidered with pearl, rends through the drawings-out of tissue, enters the linings, and skips the flesh.

CAR. I wonder he speaks not of his wrought shirt.

FAST. Here, in the opinion of mutual damage, we paused; but, ere I proceed, I must tell you, signior, that, in this last encounter, not having leisure to put off my silver spurs, one of the rowels catch'd hold of the ruffle of my boot, and, being Spanish leather, and subject to tear, overthrows me, rends me two pair of silk stockings, that I put on, being somewhat a raw morning, a peach colour and another, and strikes me some half inch deep into the side of the calf: he, seeing the blood come, presently takes horse, and away: I, having bound up my wound with a piece of my wrought shirt—

CAR. O! comes it in there?

FAST. Rid after him, and, lighting at the court gate both together, embraced, and march'dhand in hand up into the presence. Was not this business well carried?

MACI. Well! yes, and by this we can guess what apparel the gentleman wore.

PUNT. 'Fore valour, it was a designment begun with much resolution, maintain'd with as much prowess, and ended with more humanity.— RE-ENTER SERVANT. How now, what says the notary?

SERV. He says, he is ready, sir; he stays but your worship's pleasure.

PUNT. Come, we will go to him, monsieur. Gentlemen, shall we entreat you to be witnesses?

SOG. You shall entreat me, sir.—Come, Resolution.

SHIFT. I follow you, good Countenance.

CAR. Come, signior, come, come. [EXEUNT ALL BUT MACILENTE.

MACI. O, that there should be fortune To clothe these men, so naked in desert! And that the just storm of a wretched life Beats them not ragged for their wretched souls, And, since as fruitless, even as black, as coals!

[EXIT.

MIT. Why, but signior, how comes it that Fungoso appeared not with his sister's intelligence to Brisk?

COR. Marry, long of the evil angels that she gave him, who have indeed tempted the good simple youth to follow the tail of the fashion, and neglect the imposition of his friends. Behold, here he comes, very worshipfully attended, and with good variety.

SCENE V.—A ROOM IN DELIRO'S HOUSE

ENTER FUNGOSO IN A NEW SUIT, FOLLOWED BY HIS TAILOR, SHOEMAKER, AND HABERDASHER.

FUNG. Gramercy, good shoemaker, I'll put to strings myself..
        [EXIT SHOEMAKER.]—Now, sir, let me see, what must you have for this hat?

HABE. Here's the bill, sir.

FUNG. How does it become me, well?

TAI. Excellent, sir, as ever you had any hat in your life.

FUNG. Nay, you'll say so all.

HABE. In faith, sir, the hat's as good as any man in this town can serve you, and will maintain fashion as long; never trust me for a groat else.

FUNG. Does it apply well to my suit?

TAI. Exceeding well, sir.

FUNG. How lik'st thou my suit, haberdasher?

HABE. By my troth, sir, 'tis very rarely well made; I never saw a suit sit better, I can tell on.

TAI. Nay, we have no art to please our friends, we!

FUNG. Here, haberdasher, tell this same. [GIVES HIM MONEY.

HABE. Good faith, sir, it makes you have an excellent body.

FUNG. Nay, believe me, I think I have as good a body in clothes as another.

TAI. You lack points to bring your apparel together, sir.

FUNG. I'll have points anon. How now! Is't right?

HABE. Faith, sir, 'tis too little' but upon farther hopes—Good morrow to you, sir.
        [EXIT.

FUNG. Farewell, good haberdasher. Well now, master Snip, let me see your bill.

MIT. Me thinks he discharges his followers too thick.

COR. O, therein he saucily imitates some great man. I warrant you, though he turns off them, he keeps this tailor, in place of a page, to follow him still.

FUNG. This bill is very reasonable, in faith: hark you, master Snip— Troth, sir, I am not altogether so well furnished at this present, as I could wish I were; but—if you'll do me the favour to take part in hand, you shall have all I have, by this hand.

TAI. Sir—

FUNG. And but give me credit for the rest, till the beginning of the next term.

TAI. O lord, sir—

FUNG. 'Fore God, and by this light, I'll pay you to the utmost, and acknowledge myself very deeply engaged to you by the courtesy.

TAI. Why, how much have you there, sir?

FUNG. Marry, I have here four angels, and fifteen shillings of white money: it's all I have, as I hope to be blest

TAI. You will not fail me at the next term with the rest?

FUNG. No, an I do, pray heaven I be hang'd. Let me never breathe again upon this mortal stage, as the philosopher calls it! By this air, and as I am a gentleman, I'll hold.

COR. He were an iron-hearted fellow, in my judgment, that would not credit him upon this volley of oaths.

TAI. Well, sir, I'll not stick with any gentleman for a trifle: you know what 'tis remains?

FUNG. Ay, sir, and I give you thanks in good faith. O fate, how happy I am made in this good fortune! Well, now I'll go seek out monsieur Brisk. 'Ods so, I have forgot riband for my shoes, and points. 'Slid, what luck's this! how shall I do? Master Snip, pray let me reduct some two or three shillings for points and ribands:

137

as I am an honest man, I have utterly disfurnished myself, in the default of memory; pray let me be beholding to you; it shall come home in the bill, believe me.

TAI. Faith, sir, I can hardly depart with ready money; but I'll take up, and send you some by my boy presently. What coloured riband would you have?

FUNG. What you shall think meet in your judgment, sir, to my suit.

TAI. Well, I'll send you some presently.

FUNG. And points too, sir?

TAI. And points too, sir.

FUNG. Good lord, how shall I study to deserve this kindness of you sir! Pray let your youth make haste, for I should have done a business an hour since, that I doubt I shall come too late.

[EXIT TAILOR.] Now, in good faith, I am exceeding proud of my suit.

COR. Do you observe the plunges that this poor gallant is put to, signior, to purchase the fashion?

MIT. Ay, and to be still a fashion behind with the world, that's the sport.

COR. Stay: O, here they come from seal'd and deliver'd.

SCENE VI.—PUNTARVOLO'S LODGINGS.

ENTER PUNTARVOLO, FASTIDIOUS BRISK IN A
NEW SUIT, AND SERVANTS WITH THE DOG.

PUNT. Well, now my whole venture is forth, I will resolve to depart shortly.

FAST. Faith, sir Puntarvolo, go to the court, and take leave of the ladies first.

PUNT. I care not, if it be this afternoon's labour. Where is Carlo?

FAST. Here he comes.

ENTER CARLO, SOGLIARDO, SHIFT, AND MACILENTE.

CAR. Faith, gallants, I am persuading this gentleman [POINTS TO SOGLIARDO] to turn courtier. He is a man of fair revenue, and his estate will bear the charge well. Besides, for his other gifts of the mind, or so, why they are as nature lent him them, pure, simple, without any artificial drug or mixture of these two threadbare beggarly qualities, learning and knowledge, and therefore the more accommodate and genuine. Now, for the life itself—

FAST. O, the most celestial, and full of wonder and delight, that can be imagined, signior, beyond thought and apprehension of pleasure! A man lives there in that divine rapture, that he will think himself i' the ninth heaven for the time, and lose all sense of mortality whatsoever, when he shall behold such glorious, and almost immortal beauties; hear such angelical and harmonious voices, discourse with such flowing and ambrosial spirits, whose wits are as sudden as lightning, and humorous as nectar; oh, it makes a man all quintessence and flame, and lifts him up, in a moment, to the very crystal crown of the sky, where, hovering in the strength of his imagination, he shall behold all the delights of the Hesperides, the Insulae Fortunatae, Adonis' Gardens, Tempe, or what else, confined within the amplest verge of poesy, to be mere umbrae, and imperfect figures, conferred with the most essential felicity of your court.

MACI. Well, this ecomium was not extemporal, it came too perfectly off.

CAR. Besides, sir, you shall never need to go to a hot-house, you shall sweat there with courting your mistress, or losing your money at primero, as well as in all the stoves in Sweden. Marry, this, sir, you must ever be sure to carry a good strong perfume about you, that your mistress's dog may smell you out amongst the rest; and, in making love to her, never fear to be out; for you may have a pipe of tobacco, or a bass viol shall hang o' the wall, of purpose, will put you in presently. The tricks your Resolution has taught you in tobacco, the whiffe, and those sleights, will stand you in very good ornament there.

FAST. Ay, to some, perhaps; but, an he should come to my mistress with tobacco (this gentleman knows) she'd reply upon him, i'faith. O, by this bright sun, she has the most acute, ready, and facetious wit that—tut, there's no spirit able to stand her. You can report it, signior, you have seen her.

PUNT. Then can he report no less, out of his judgment, I assure him.

MACI. Troth, I like her well enough, but she's too self-conceited, methinks.

FAST. Ay, indeed, she's a little too self-conceited; an 'twere not for that humour, she were the most-to-be-admired lady in the world.

PUNT. Indeed, it is a humour that takes from her other excellences.

MACI. Why, it may easily be made to forsake her, in my thought.

FAST. Easily, sir! then are all impossibilities easy.

MACI. You conclude too quick upon me, signior. What will you say, if I make it so perspicuously appear now, that yourself shall confess nothing more possible?

FAST. Marry, I will say, I will both applaud and admire you for it.

PUNT. And I will second him in the admiration.

MACI. Why, I'll show you, gentlemen.—Carlo, come hither. [MACI., CAR., PUNT., AND FAST. WHISPER TOGETHER.

SOG. Good faith, I have a great humour to the court. What thinks my Resolution? shall I adventure?

SHIFT. Troth, Countenance, as you please; the place is a place of good reputation and capacity.

SOG. O, my tricks in tobacco, as Carlo says, will show excellent there.

SHIFT. Why, you may go with these gentlemen now, and see fashions; and after, as you shall see correspondence.

SOG. You say true. You will go with me, Resolution?

SHIFT. I will meet you, Countenance, about three or four o'clock; but, to say to go with you, I cannot; for, as I am Apple-John, I am to go before the cockatrice you saw this morning, and therefore pray, present me excused, good Countenance.

SOG. Farewell, good Resolution, but fail not to meet.

SHIFT. As I live.
                    [EXIT.

PUNT. Admirably excellent!

MACI. If you can but persuade Sogliardo to court, there's all now.

CAR. O, let me alone, that's my task. [GOES TO SOGLIARDO.

FAST. Now, by wit, Macilente, it's above measure excellent; 'twill be the only court-exploit that ever proved courtier ingenious.

PUNT. Upon my soul, it puts the lady quite out of her humour, and we shall laugh with judgment.

CAR. Come, the gentleman was of himself resolved to go with you, afore I moved it.

MACI. Why, then, gallants, you two and Carlo go afore to prepare the jest; Sogliardo and I will come some while after you.

CAR. Pardon me, I am not for the court.

PUNT. That's true; Carlo comes not at court, indeed. Well, you shall leave it to the faculty of monsieur Brisk, and myself; upon our lives, we will manage it happily. Carlo shall bespeak supper at the Mitre, against we come back: where we will meet and dimple our cheeks with laughter at the success.

CAR. Ay, but will you promise to come?

PUNT. Myself shall undertake for them; he that fails, let his reputation lie under the lash of thy tongue.

CAR. Ods so, look who comes here!
        ENTER FUNGOSO.

141

SOG. What, nephew!

FUNG. Uncle, God save you; did you see a gentleman, one monsieur Brisk, a courtier? he goes in such a suit as I do.

SOG. Here is the gentleman, nephew, but not in such a suit.

FUNG. Another suit!

SOG. How now, nephew?

FAST. Would you speak with me, sir?

CAR. Ay, when he has recovered himself, poor Poll!

PUNT. Some rosa-solis.

MACI. How now, signior?

FUNG. I am not well, sir.

MACI. Why, this it is to dog the fashion.

CAR. Nay, come, gentlemen, remember your affairs; his disease is nothing but the flux of apparel.

PUNT. Sirs, return to the lodging, keep the cat safe; I'll be the dog's guardian myself. [EXEUNT SERVANTS.

SOG. Nephew, will you go to court with us? these gentlemen and I are for the court; nay, be not so melancholy.

FUNG. 'Slid, I think no man in Christendom has that rascally fortune that I have.

MACI. Faith, you suit is well enough, signior.

FUNG. Nay, not for that, I protest; but I had an errand to monsieur Fastidious, and I have forgot it.

MACI. Why, go along to court with us, and remember it; come, gentlemen, you three take one boat, and Sogliardo and I will take another; we shall be there instantly.

FAST. Content: good sir, vouchsafe us your pleasance.

PUNT. Farewell, Carlo: remember.

CAR. I warrant you: would I had one of Kemp's shoes to throw after you.

PUNT. Good fortune will close the eyes of our jest, fear not; and we shall frolick. [EXEUNT.

MIT. This Macilente, signior, begins to be more sociable on a sudden, methinks, than he was before: there's some portent in it, I believe.

COR. O, he's a fellow of a strange nature. Now does he, in this calm of his humour, plot, and store up a world of malicious thoughts in his brain, till he is so full with them, that you shall see the very torrent of his envy break forth like a land-flood: and, against the course of all their affections, oppose itself so violently, that you will almost have wonder to think, how 'tis possible the current of their dispositions shall receive so quick and strong an alteration.

MIT. Ay, marry, sir, this is that, on which my expectation has dwelt all this while; for I must tell you, signior, though I was loth to interrupt the scene, yet I made it a question in mine own private discourse, how he should properly call it "Every Man out of his Humour", when I saw all his actors so strongly pursue, and continue their humours?

COR. Why, therein his art appears most full of lustre, and approacheth nearest the life; especially when in the flame and height of their humours, they are laid flat, it fills the eye better, and with more contentment. How tedious a sight were it to behold a proud exalted tree kept and cut down by degrees, when it might be fell'd in a moment! and to set the axe to it before it came to that pride and fulness, were, as not to have it grow.

MIT. Well, I shall long till I see this fall, you talk of.

COR. To help your longing, signior, let your imagination be swifter than a pair of oars: and by this, suppose Puntarvolo, Brisk, Fungoso, and the dog, arrived at the court-gate, and going up to the great chamber. Macilente and Sogliardo, we'll leave them on the water, till possibility and natural means may land them. Here come the gallants, now prepare your expectations.

ACT V

SCENE I.—THE PALACE STAIRS.

ENTER PUNTARVOLO, WITH HIS DOG, FOLLOWED BY FASTIDIOUS BRISK AND FUNGOSO.

PUNT. Come, gentles, Signior, you are sufficiently instructed.

FAST. Who, I, sir?

PUNT. No, this gentleman. But stay, I take thought how to bestow my dog; he is no competent attendant for the presence.

FAST. Mass, that's true, indeed, knight; you must not carry him into the presence.

PUNT. I know it, and I, like a dull beast, forgot to bring one of my cormorants to attend me.

FAST. Why, you were best leave him at the porter's lodge.

PUNT. Not so; his worth is too well known amongst them, to be forthcoming.

FAST. 'Slight, how will you do then?

PUNT. I must leave him with one that is ignorant of his quality, if I will have him to be safe. And see! here comes one that will carry coals, ergo, will hold my dog. ENTER A GROOM, WITH A BASKET. My honest friend, may I commit the tuition of this dog to thy prudent care?

GROOM. You may, if you please, sir.

PUNT. Pray thee let me find thee here at my return; it shall not be long, till I will ease thee of thy employment, and please thee. Forth, gentles.

FAST. Why, but will you leave him with so slight command, and infuse no more charge upon the fellow?

PUNT. Charge! no; there were no policy in that; that were to let him know the value of the gem he holds, and so to tempt frail nature

144

against her disposition. No, pray thee let thy honesty be sweet, as it shall be short.

GROOM. Yes, sir.

PUNT. But hark you, gallants, and chiefly monsieur Brisk: when we come in eye-shot, or presence of this lady, let not other matters carry us from our project; but, if we can, single her forth to some place—

FAST. I warrant you.

PUNT. And be not too sudden, but let the device induce itself with good circumstance. On.

FUNG. Is this the way? good truth, here be fine hangings. [EXEUNT PUNT., FAST., AND FUNGOSO.

GROOM. Honesty! sweet, and short! Marry, it shall, sir, doubt you not; for even at this instant if one would give me twenty pounds, I would not deliver him; there's for the sweet: but now, if any man come offer me but two-pence, he shall have him; there's for the short now. 'Slid, what a mad humorous gentleman is this to leave his dog with me! I could run away with him now, an he were worth any thing.

ENTER MACILENTE AND SOGLIARDO. MACI. Come on, signior, now prepare to court this all-witted lady, most naturally, and like yourself.

SOG. Faith, an you say the word, I'll begin to her in tobacco.

MACI. O, fie on't! no; you shall begin with, "How does my sweet lady", or, "Why are you so melancholy, madam?" though she be very merry, it's all one. Be sure to kiss your hand often enough; pray for her health, and tell her, how "More than most fair she is". Screw your face at one side thus, and protest: let her fleer, and look askance, and hide her teeth with her fan, when she laughs a fit, to bring her into more matter, that's nothing: you must talk forward, (though it be without sense, so it be without blushing,) 'tis most court-like and well.

SOG. But shall I not use tobacco at all?

MACI. O, by no means; 'twill but make your breath suspected, and that you use it only to confound the rankness of that.

SOG. Nay, I'll be advised, sir, by my friends.

MACI. Od's my life, see where sir Puntarvolo's dog is.

GROOM. I would the gentleman would return for his follower here, I'll
leave him to his fortunes else.

MACI. 'Twere the only true jest in the world to poison him now; ha! by this
hand I'll do it, if I could but get him of the fellow. [ASIDE.] Signior
Sogliardo, walk aside, and think upon some device to entertain the
lady with.

SOG. So I do, sir. [WALKS OFF IN A MEDITATING POSTURE.

MACI. How now, mine honest friend! whose dog-keeper art thou?

GROOM. Dog-keeper, sir! I hope I scorn that, i'faith.

MACI. Why, dost thou not keep a dog?

GROOM. Sir, now I do, and now I do not: [THROWS OFF THE DOG.] I
think this be sweet and short. Make me his dog-keeper!
                            [EXIT.

MACI. This is excellent, above expectation! nay, stay, sir; [SEIZING THE
DOG.] you'd be travelling; but I'll give you a dram shall shorten your
voyage, here. [GIVES HIM POISON.] So, sir, I'll be bold to take
my leave of you. Now to the Turk's court in the devil's name, for
you shall never go o' God's name. [KICKS HIM OUT.]—Sogliardo,
come.

SOG. I have it i'faith now, will sting it.

MACI. Take heed you leese it not signior, ere you come there; preserve
it. [EXEUNT.

COR. How like you this first exploit of his?

MIT. O, a piece of true envy; but I expect the issue of the other device.

COR. Here they come will make it appear.

SCENE II.—AN APARTMENT IN THE PALACE.

ENTER SAVIOLINA, PUNTARVOLO, FASTIDIOUS BRISK, AND FUNGOSO.

SAV. Why, I thought, sir Puntarvolo, you had been gone your voyage?

PUNT. Dear and most amiable lady, your divine beauties do bind me to those offices, that I cannot depart when I would.

SAV. 'Tis most court-like spoken, sir; but how might we do to have a sight of your dog and cat?

FAST. His dog is in the court, lady.

SAV. And not your cat? how dare you trust her behind you, sir.

PUNT. Troth, madam, she hath sore eyes, and she doth keep her chamber; marry, I have left her under sufficient guard there are two of my followers to attend her.

SAV. I'll give you some water for her eyes. When do you go, sir?

PUNT. Certes, sweet lady, I know not.

FAST. He doth stay the rather, madam, to present your acute judgment with so courtly and well parted a gentleman as yet your ladyship hath never seen.

SAV. What is he, gentle monsieur Brisk? not that gentleman? [POINTS TO FUNGOSO.

FAST. No, lady, this is a kinsman to justice Silence.

PUNT. Pray, sir, give me leave to report him. He's a gentleman, lady, of that rare and admirable faculty, as, I protest, I know not his like in Europe; he is exceedingly valiant, an excellent scholar, and so exactly travelled, that he is able, in discourse, to deliver you a model of any prince's court in the world; speaks the languages with that purity of phrase, and facility of accent, that it breeds astonishment; his wit, the most exuberant, and, above wonder, pleasant, of all that ever entered the concave of this ear.

FAST. 'Tis most true, lady; marry, he is no such excellent proper man.

PUNT. His travels have changed his complexion, madam.

SAV. O, sir Puntarvolo, you must think every man was not born to have my servant Brisk's feature.

PUNT. But that which transcends all, lady; he doth so peerlessly imitate any manner of person for gesture, action, passion, or whatever—

FAST. Ay, especially a rustic or a clown, madam, that it is not possible for the sharpest-sighted wit in the world to discern any sparks of the gentleman in him, when he does it.

SAV. O, monsieur Brisk, be not so tyrannous to confine all wits within the compass of your own; not find the sparks of a gentleman in him, if he be a gentleman!

FUNG. No, in truth, sweet lady, I believe you cannot.

SAV. Do you believe so? why, I can find sparks of a gentleman in you, sir.

PUNT. Ay, he is a gentleman, madam, and a reveller.

FUNG. Indeed, I think I have seen your ladyship at our revels.

SAV. Like enough, sir; but would I might see this wonder you talk of; may one have a sight of him for any reasonable sum?

PUNT. Yes, madam, he will arrive presently.

SAV. What, and shall we see him clown it?

FAST. I'faith, sweet lady, that you shall; see, here he comes.

ENTER MACILENTE AND SOGLIARDO. PUNT. This is he! pray observe him, lady.

SAV. Beshrew me, he clowns it properly indeed.

PUNT. Nay, mark his courtship.

SOG. How does my sweet lady? hot and moist? beautiful and lusty? ha!

SAV. Beautiful, an it please you, sir, but not lusty.

148

SOG. O ho, lady, it pleases you to say so, in truth: And how does my sweet lady? in health? 'Bonaroba, quaeso, que novelles? que novelles?' sweet creature!

SAV. O excellent! why, gallants, is this he that cannot be deciphered? they were very blear-witted, i'faith, that could not discern the gentleman in him.

PUNT. But you do, in earnest, lady?

SAV. Do I sir! why, if you had any true court-judgment in the carriage of his eye, and that inward power that forms his countenance, you might perceive his counterfeiting as clear as the noon-day; alas—nay, if you would have tried my wit, indeed, you should never have told me he was a gentleman, but presented him for a true clown indeed; and then have seen if I could have deciphered him.

FAST. 'Fore God, her ladyship says true, knight: but does he not affect the clown most naturally, mistress?

PUNT. O, she cannot but affirm that, out of the bounty of her judgment.

SAV. Nay, out of doubt he does well, for a gentleman to imitate: but I warrant you, he becomes his natural carriage of the gentleman, much better than his clownery.

FAST. 'Tis strange, in truth, her ladyship should see so far into him!

PUNT. Ay, is it not?

SAV. Faith, as easily as may be; not decipher him, quoth you!

FUNG. Good sadness, I wonder at it

MACI. Why, has she deciphered him, gentlemen?

PUNT. O, most miraculously, and beyond admiration.

MACI. Is it possible?

FAST. She hath gather'd most infallible signs of the gentleman in him, that's certain.

SAV. Why, gallants, let me laugh at you a little: was this your device, to try my judgment in a gentleman?

149

MACI. Nay, lady, do not scorn us, though you have this gift of perspicacy above others. What if he should be no gentleman now, but a clown indeed, lady?

PUNT. How think you of that? would not your ladyship be Out of your Humour?

FAST. O, but she knows it is not so.

SAV. What if he were not a man, ye may as well say? Nay, if your worships could gull me so, indeed, you were wiser than you are taken for.

MACI. In good faith, lady, he is a very perfect clown, both by father and mother; that I'll assure you.

SAV. O, sir, you are very pleasurable.

MACI. Nay, do but look on his hand, and that shall resolve you; look you, lady, what a palm here is.

SOG. Tut, that was with holding the plough.

MACI. The plough! did you discern any such thing in him, madam?

FAST. Faith no, she saw the gentleman as bright as noon-day, she; she deciphered him at first.

MACI. Troth, I am sorry your ladyship's sight should be so suddenly struck.

SAV. O, you are goodly beagles!

FAST. What, is she gone?

SOG. Nay, stay, sweet lady: 'que novelles? que novelles?'

SAV. Out, you fool, you!

[EXIT IN ANGER.

FUNG. She's Out of her Humour, i'faith.

FAST. Nay, let's follow it while 'tis hot, gentlemen.

PUNT. Come, on mine honour we shall make her blush in the presence; my spleen is great with laughter.

MACI. Your laughter will be a child of a feeble life, I believe, sir. [ASIDE.]—Come, signior, your looks are too dejected, methinks; why mix you not mirth with the rest?

150

FUNG. Od's will, this suit frets me at the soul. I'll have it alter'd tomorrow, sure.

SCENE III.—THE PALACE STAIRS.

ENTER SHIFT.

SHIFT. I am come to the court, to meet with my Countenance, Sogliardo; poor men must be glad of such countenance, when they can get no better. Well, need may insult upon a man, but it shall never make him despair of consequence. The world will say, 'tis base: tush, base! 'tis base to live under the earth, not base to live above it by any means.

ENTER FASTIDIOUS, PUNTARVOLO, SOGLIARDO, FUNGOSO, AND MACILENTE. FAST. The poor lady is most miserably out of her humour, i'faith.

PUNT. There was never so witty a jest broken, at the tilt of all the court wits christen'd.

MACI. O, this applause taints it foully.

SOG. I think I did my part in courting.—O, Resolution!

PUNT. Ay me, my dog!

MACI. Where is he?

FAST. 'Sprecious, go seek for the fellow, good signior
            [EXIT FUNGOSO.

PUNT. Here, here I left him.

MACI. Why, none was here when we came in now, but cavalier Shift; enquire of him.

FAST. Did you see sir Puntarvolo's dog here, cavalier, since you came?

SHIFT. His dog, sir! he may look his dog, sir; I saw none of his dog, sir.

MACI. Upon my life, he has stolen your dog, sir, and been hired to it by some that have ventured with you; you may guess by his peremptory answers.

151

PUNT. Not unlike; for he hath been a notorious thief by his own confession. Sirrah, where is my dog?

SHIFT. Charge me with your dog, sir! I have none of your dog, sir.

PUNT. Villain, thou liest.

SHIFT. Lie, sir! s'blood,—you are but a man, sir.

PUNT. Rogue and thief, restore him.

SOG. Take heed, sir Puntarvolo, what you do; he'll bear no coals, I can tell you, o' my word.

MACI. This is rare.

SOG. It's marle he stabs you not: By this light, he hath stabbed forty, for forty times less matter, I can tell you of my knowledge.

PUNT. I will make thee stoop, thou abject.

SOG. Make him stoop, sir! Gentlemen, pacify him, or he'll be kill'd.

MACI. Is he so tall a man?

SOG. Tall a man! if you love his life, stand betwixt them. Make him stoop!

PUNT. My dog, villain, or I will hang thee; thou hast confest robberies, and other felonious acts, to this gentleman, thy Countenance—

SOG. I'll bear no witness.

PUNT. And without my dog, I will hang thee, for them. [SHIFT KNEELS.

SOG. What! kneel to thine enemies!

SHIFT. Pardon me, good sir; God is my witness, I never did robbery in all my life.

RE-ENTER FUNGOSO. FUNG. O, sir Puntarvolo, your dog lies giving up the ghost in the wood-yard.

MACI. Heart, is he not dead yet! [ASIDE.

PUNT. O, my dog, born to disastrous fortune! pray you conduct me, sir.

[EXIT WITH FUNGOSO.

SOG. How! did you never do any robbery in your life?

MACI. O, this is good! so he swore, sir.

152

SOG. Ay, I heard him: and did you swear true, sir?

SHIFT. Ay, as I hope to be forgiven, sir, I never robbed any man; I never stood by the highwayside, sir, but only said so, because I would get myself a name, and be counted a tall man.

SOG. Now out, base viliaco! thou my Resolution! I thy Countenance! By this light, gentlemen, he hath confest to me the most inexorable company of robberies, and damn'd himself that he did 'em: you never heard the like. Out, scoundrel, out! follow me no more, I command thee; out of my sight, go, hence, speak not; I will not hear thee: away, camouccio!

[EXIT SHIFT.

MACI. O, how I do feed upon this now, and fat myself! here were a couple unexpectedly dishumour'd. Well, by this time, I hope, sir Puntarvolo and his dog are both out of humour to travel. [ASIDE.]—Nay, gentlemen, why do you not seek out the knight, and comfort him? our supper at the Mitre must of necessity hold tonight, if you love your reputations.

FAST. 'Fore God, I am so melancholy for his dog's disaster—but I'll go.

SOG. Faith, and I may go too, but I know I shall be so melancholy.

MACI. Tush, melancholy! you must forget that now, and remember you lie at the mercy of a fury: Carlo will rack your sinews asunder, and rail you to dust, if you come not. [EXEUNT.

MIT. O, then their fear of Carlo, belike, makes them hold their meeting.

COR. Ay, here he comes; conceive him but to be enter'd the Mitre, and 'tis enough.

SCENE IV.—A ROOM AT THE MITRE.

ENTER CARLO. CAR. Holla! where be these shot-sharks?
    ENTER DRAWER.
    DRAW. By and by; you are welcome, good master Buffone.
CAR. Where's George? call me George hither, quickly.

153

DRAW. What wine please you have, sir? I'll draw you that's neat, master Buffone.

CAR. Away, neophite, do as I bid thee, bring my dear George to me:— ENTER GEORGE. Mass, here he comes.

GEORGE. Welcome, master Carlo.

CAR. What, is supper ready, George?

GEORGE. Ay, sir, almost: Will you have the cloth laid, master Carlo?

CAR. O, what else? Are none of the gallants come yet?

GEORGE. None yet, sir.

CAR. Stay, take me with you, George; let me have a good fat loin of pork laid to the fire, presently.

GEORGE. It shall, sir.

CAR. And withal, hear you, draw me the biggest shaft you have out of the butt you wot of; away, you know my meaning, George; quick!

GEORGE. Done, sir.

[EXIT.

CAR. I never hungered so much for anything in my life, as I do to know our gallants' success at court; now is that lean, bald-rib Macilente, that salt villain, plotting some mischievous device, and lies a soaking in their frothy humours like a dry crust, till he has drunk 'em all up: Could the pummice but hold up his eyes at other men's happiness, in any reasonable proportion, 'slid, the slave were to be loved next heaven, above honour, wealth, rich fare, apparel, wenches, all the delights of the belly and the groin, whatever.

RE-ENTER GEORGE WITH TWO JUGS OF WINE. GEORGE. Here, master Carlo.

CAR. Is it right, boy?

GEORGE. Ay, sir, I assure you 'tis right.

CAR. Well said, my dear George, depart:

[EXIT GEORGE.]—Come, my small gimblet, you in the false scabbard, away, so! [PUTS FORTH THE DRAWER,

154

AND SHUTS THE DOOR.] Now to you, sir Burgomaster, let's taste of your bounty.

MIT. What, will he deal upon such quantities of wine, alone?

COR. You will perceive that, sir.

CAR. [DRINKS.] Ay, marry, sir, here's purity; O, George—I could bite off his nose for this now, sweet rogue, he has drawn nectar, the very soul of the grape! I'll wash my temples with some on't presently, and drink some half a score draughts; 'twill heat the brain, kindle my imagination, I shall talk nothing but crackers and fire-works tonight. So, sir! please you to be here, sir, and I here: so. [SETS THE TWO CUPS ASUNDER, DRINKS WITH THE ONE, AND PLEDGES WITH THE OTHER, SPEAKING FOR EACH OF THE CUPS, AND DRINKING ALTERNATELY.

COR. This is worth the observation, signior.

CAR. 1 CUP. Now, sir, here's to you; and I present you with so much of my love.

2 CUP. I take it kindly from you, sir. [DRINKS], and will return you the like proportion; but withal, sir, remembering the merry night we had at the countess's, you know where, sir.

1 CUP. By heaven, you put me in mind now of a very necessary office, which I will propose in your pledge, sir; the health of that honourable countess, and the sweet lady that sat by her, sir.

2 CUP. I do vail to it with reverence [DRINKS]. And now, signior, with these ladies, I'll be bold to mix the health of your divine mistress.

1 CUP. Do you know her, sir?

2 CUP. O lord, sir, ay; and in the respectful memory and mention of her, I could wish this wine were the most precious drug in the world.

1 CUP. Good faith, sir, you do honour me in't exceedingly. [DRINKS.]

MIT. Whom should he personate in this, signior?

COR. Faith, I know not, sir; observe, observe him.

2 CUP. If it were the basest filth, or mud that runs in the channel, I am bound to pledge it respectively, sir. [DRINKS.] And now, sir, here

155

is a replenish'd bowl, which I will reciprocally turn upon you, to the health of the count Frugale.

1 CUP. The count Frugale's health, sir? I'll pledge it on my knees, by this light. [KNEELS.

2 CUP. Nay, do me right, sir.

1 CUP. So I do, in faith.

2 CUP. Good faith you do not; mine was fuller.

1 CUP. Why, believe me, it was not.

2 CUP. Believe me it was; and you do lie.

1 CUP. Lie, sir!

2 CUP. Ay, sir.

1 CUP. 'Swounds! you rascal!

2 CUP. O, come, stab if you have a mind to it.

1 CUP. Stab! dost thou think I dare not?

CAR. [SPEAKS IN HIS OWN PERSON.] Nay, I beseech you, gentlemen, what means this? nay, look, for shame respect your reputations. [OVERTURNS WINE, POT, CUPS, AND ALL.

ENTER MACILENTE. MACI. Why, how now, Carlo! what humour's this?

CAR. O, my good mischief! art thou come? where are the rest, where are the rest?

MACI. Faith, three of our ordnance are burst.

CAR. Burst! how comes that?

MACI. Faith, overcharged, overcharged.

CAR. But did not the train hold?

MACI. O, yes, and the poor lady is irrecoverably blown up.

CAR. Why, but which of the munition is miscarried, ha?

MACI. Imprimis, sir Puntarvolo; next, the Countenance and Resolution.

CAR. How, how, for the love of wit?

MACI. Troth, the Resolution is proved recreant; the Countenance hath changed his copy; and the passionate knight is shedding funeral tears over his departed dog.

156

CAR. What! is his dog dead?

MACI. Poison'd, 'tis thought; marry, how, or by whom, that's left for some cunning woman here o' the Bank-side to resolve. For my part, I know nothing more than that we are like to have an exceeding melancholy supper of it.

CAR. 'Slife, and I had purposed to be extraordinarily merry, I had drunk off a good preparative of old sack here; but will they come, will they come?

MACI. They will assuredly come; marry, Carlo, as thou lov'st me, run over 'em all freely tonight, and especially the knight; spare no sulphurous jest that may come out of that sweaty forge of thine; but ply them with all manner of shot, minion, saker, culverin, or anything, what thou wilt.

CAR. I warrant thee, my dear case of petrionels; so I stand not in dread of thee, but that thou'lt second me.

MACI. Why, my good German tapster, I will.

CAR. What George! Lomtero, Lomtero, etc. [SINGS AND DANCES.

RE-ENTER GEORGE. GEORGE. Did you call, master Carlo?

CAR. More nectar, George: Lomtero, etc.

GEORGE. Your meat's ready, sir, an your company were come.

CAR. Is the loin pork enough?

GEORGE. Ay, sir, it is enough.

[EXIT.

MACI. Pork! heart, what dost thou with such a greasy dish? I think thou dost varnish thy face with the fat on't, it looks so like a glue-pot.

CAR. True, my raw-boned rogue, and if thou wouldst farce thy lean ribs with it too, they would not, like ragged laths, rub out so many doublets as they do; but thou know'st not a good dish, thou. O, it's the only nourishing meat in the world. No marvel though that saucy, stubborn generation, the Jews, were forbidden it; for what would they have done, well pamper'd with fat pork, that durst murmur at their Maker out of garlick and onions? 'Slight! fed with it, the

157

whoreson strummel-patch'd, goggle-eyed grumble-dories, would have gigantomachised—RE-ENTER GEORGE WITH WINE. Well said, my sweet George, fill, fill.

MIT. This savours too much of profanation.

COR. O—Servetur ad imum, Qualis ab incoepto processerit, et sibi constet. "The necessity of his vein compels a toleration, for; bar this, and dash him out of humour before his time."

CAR. "'Tis an axiom in natural philosophy, what comes nearest the nature of that it feeds, converts quicker to nourishment, and doth sooner essentiate." Now nothing in flesh and entrails assimilates or resembles man more than a hog or swine. [DRINKS.

MACI. True; and he, to requite their courtesy, oftentimes doffeth his own nature, and puts on theirs; as when he becomes as churlish as a hog, or as drunk as a sow; but to your conclusion. [DRINKS.

CAR. Marry, I say, nothing resembling man more than a swine, it follows, nothing can be more nourishing; for indeed (but that it abhors from our nice nature) if we fed upon one another, we should shoot up a great deal faster, and thrive much better; I refer me to your usurous cannibals, or such like; but since it is so contrary, pork, pork, is your only feed.

MACI. I take it, your devil be of the same diet; he would never have desired to have been incorporated into swine else.—O, here comes the melancholy mess; upon 'em, Carlo, charge, charge!

ENTER PUNTARVOLO, FASTIDIOUS BRISK, SOGLIARDO, AND FUNGOSO. CAR. 'Fore God, sir Puntarvolo, I am sorry for your heaviness: body o' me, a shrew'd mischance! why, had you no unicorn's horn, nor bezoar's stone about you, ha?

PUNT. Sir, I would request you be silent.

MACI. Nay, to him again.

CAR. Take comfort, good knight, if your cat have recovered her catarrh, fear nothing; your dog's mischance may be holpen.

FAST. Say how, sweet Carlo; for, so God mend me, the poor knight's moans draw me into fellowship of his misfortunes. But be not discouraged, good sir Puntarvolo, I am content your adventure shall be performed upon your cat.

MACI. I believe you, musk-cod, I believe you; for rather than thou would'st make present repayment, thou would'st take it upon his own bare return from Calais [ASIDE.

CAR. Nay, 'slife, he'd be content, so he were well rid out of his company, to pay him five for one, at his next meeting him in Paul's. [ASIDE TO MACILENTE.]—But for your dog, sir Puntarvolo, if he be not out-right dead, there is a friend of mine, a quack-salver, shall put life in him again, that's certain.

FUNG. O, no, that comes too late.

MACI. 'Sprecious! knight, will you suffer this?

PUNT. Drawer, get me a candle and hard wax presently.

                    [EXIT GEORGE.

SOG. Ay, and bring up supper; for I am so melancholy.

CAR. O, signior, where's your Resolution?

SOG. Resolution! hang him, rascal: O, Carlo, if you love me, do not mention him.

CAR. Why, how so?

SOG. O, the arrantest crocodile that ever Christian was acquainted with. By my gentry, I shall think the worse of tobacco while I live, for his sake: I did think him to be as tall a man—

MACI. Nay, Buffone, the knight, the knight [ASIDE TO CARLO.

CAR. 'Slud, he looks like an image carved out of box, full of knots; his face is, for all the world, like a Dutch purse, with the mouth downward, his beard the tassels; and he walks—let me see—as melancholy as one o' the master's side in the Counter.—Do you hear, sir Puntarvolo?

PUNT. Sir, I do entreat you, no more, but enjoin you to silence, as you affect your peace.

159

CAR. Nay, but dear knight, understand here are none but friends, and such as wish you well, I would have you do this now; flay me your dog presently (but in any case keep the head) and stuff his skin well with straw, as you see these dead monsters at Bartholomew fair.

PUNT. I shall be sudden, I tell you.

CAR. O, if you like not that, sir, get me somewhat a less dog, and clap into the skin; here's a slave about the town here, a Jew, one Yohan: or a fellow that makes perukes will glue it on artificially, it shall never be discern'd; besides, 'twill be so much the warmer for the hound to travel in, you know.

MACI. Sir Puntarvolo, death, can you be so patient!

CAR. Or thus, sir; you may have, as you come through Germany, a familiar for little or nothing, shall turn itself into the shape of your dog, or any thing, what you will, for certain hours—[PUNTARVOLO STRIKES HIM]—Ods my life, knight, what do you mean? you'll offer no violence, will you? hold, hold!

RE-ENTER GEORGE, WITH WAX, AND A LIGHTED CANDLE.

PUNT. 'Sdeath, you slave, you ban-dog, you!

CAR. As you love wit, stay the enraged knight, gentlemen.

PUNT. By my knighthood, he that stirs in his rescue, dies.—Drawer, begone!

[EXIT GEORGE.

CAR. Murder, murder, murder!

PUNT. Ay, are you howling, you wolf?—Gentlemen, as you tender your lives, suffer no man to enter till my revenge be perfect. Sirrah, Buffone, lie down; make no exclamations, but down; down, you cur, or I will make thy blood flow on my rapier hilts.

CAR. Sweet knight, hold in thy fury, and 'fore heaven I'll honour thee more than the Turk does Mahomet.

PUNT. Down, I say! [CARLO LIES DOWN.]—Who's there? [KNOCKING WITHIN.

CONS. [WITHIN.] Here's the constable, open the doors.

CAR. Good Macilente—

PUNT. Open no door; if the Adalantado of Spain were here he should not enter: one help me with the light, gentlemen; you knock in vain, sir officer.

CAR. 'Et tu, Brute!'

PUNT. Sirrah, close your lips, or I will drop it in thine eyes, by heaven.

CAR. O! O!

CONS. [WITHIN] Open the door, or I will break it open.

MACI. Nay, good constable, have patience a little; you shall come in presently; we have almost done. [PUNTARVOLO SEALS UP CARLO'S LIPS.

PUNT. So, now, are you Out of your Humour, sir? Shift, gentlemen [THEY ALL DRAW, AND RUN OUT, EXCEPT FUNGOSO, WHO CONCEALS HIMSELF BENEATH THE TABLE. ENTER CONSTABLE AND OFFICERS, AND SEIZE FASTIDIOUS AS HE IS RUSHING BY. CONS. Lay hold upon this gallant, and pursue the rest.

FAST. Lay hold on me, sir, for what?

CONS. Marry, for your riot here, sir, with the rest of your companions.

FAST. My riot! master constable, take heed what you do. Carlo, did I offer any violence?

CONS. O, sir, you see he is not in case to answer you, and that makes you so peremptory.

RE-ENTER GEORGE AND DRAWER. FAST. Peremptory! 'Slife, I appeal to the drawers, if I did him any hard measure.

GEORGE. They are all gone, there's none of them will be laid any hold on.

CONS. Well, sir, you are like to answer till the rest can be found out.

FAST. 'Slid, I appeal to George here.

CONS. Tut, George was not here: away with him to the Counter, sirs.— Come, sir, you were best get yourself drest somewhere. [EXEUNT CONST. AND OFFICERS, WITH FAST. AND CAR.

GEORGE. Good lord, that master Carlo could not take heed, and knowing what a gentleman the knight is, if he be angry.

    DRAWER. A pox on 'em, they have left all the meat on our hands; would they were choaked with it for me!

RE-ENTER MACILENTE. MACI. What, are they gone, sirs?

GEORGE. O, here's master Macilente.

MACI. [POINTING TO FUNGOSO.] Sirrah, George, do you see that concealment there, that napkin under the table?

GEORGE. 'Ods so, signior Fungoso!

MACI. He's good pawn for the reckoning; be sure you keep him here, and let him not go away till I come again, though he offer to discharge all; I'll return presently.

GEORGE. Sirrah, we have a pawn for the reckoning.

    DRAW. What, of Macilente?

GEORGE. No; look under the table.

FUNG. [CREEPING OUT.] I hope all be quiet now; if I can get but forth of this street, I care not: masters, I pray you tell me, is the constable gone?

GEORGE. What, master Fungoso!

FUNG. Was't not a good device this same of me, sirs?

GEORGE. Yes, faith; have you been here all this while?

FUNG. O lord, ay; good sir, look an the coast be clear, I'd fain be going.

GEORGE. All's clear, sir, but the reckoning; and that you must clear and pay before you go, I assure you.

FUNG. I pay! 'Slight, I eat not a bit since I came into the house, yet.

    DRAW. Why, you may when you please, 'tis all ready below that was bespoken.

FUNG. Bespoken! not by me, I hope?

162

GEORGE. By you, sir! I know not that; but 'twas for you and your company, I am sure.

FUNG. My company! 'Slid, I was an invited guest, so I was.

    DRAW. Faith we have nothing to do with that, sir: they are all gone but you, and we must be answered; that's the short and the long on't.

FUNG. Nay, if you will grow to extremities, my masters, then would this pot, cup, and all were in my belly, if I have a cross about me.

GEORGE. What, and have such apparel! do not say so, signior; that mightily discredits your clothes.

FUNG. As I am an honest man, my tailor had all my money this morning, and yet I must be fain to alter my suit too. Good sirs, let me go, 'tis Friday night, and in good truth I have no stomach in the world to eat any thing.

    DRAW. That's no matter, so you pay, sir.

FUNG. 'Slight, with what conscience can you ask me to pay that I never drank for?

GEORGE. Yes, sir, I did see you drink once.

FUNG. By this cup, which is silver, but you did not; you do me infinite wrong: I looked in the pot once, indeed, but I did not drink.

    DRAW. Well, sir, if you can satisfy our master, it shall be all one to us.

    WITHIN. George!

GEORGE. By and by. [EXEUNT.

COR. Lose not yourself now, signior

SCENE V.—A ROOM IN DELIRO'S HOUSE.

ENTER MACILENTE AND DELIRO.

MACI. Tut, sir, you did bear too hard a conceit of me in that; but I will not make my love to you most transparent, in spite of any dust of suspicion that may be raised to cloud it; and henceforth, since I see it is so against your humour, I will never labour to persuade you.

DELI. Why, I thank you, signior; but what is that you tell me may concern my peace so much?

MACI. Faith, sir, 'tist hus. Your wife's brother, signior Fungoso, being at supper tonight at a tavern, with a sort of gallants, there happened some division amongst them, and he is left in pawn for the reckoning. Now, if ever you look that time shall present you with an happy occasion to do your wife some gracious and acceptable service, take hold of this opportunity, and presently go and redeem him; for, being her brother, and his credit so amply engaged as now it is, when she shall hear, (as he cannot himself, but he must out of extremity report it,) that you came, and offered y ourself so kindly, and with that respect of his reputation; why, the benefit cannot but make her dote, and grow mad of your affections.

DELI. Now, by heaven, Macilente, I acknowledge myself exceedingly indebted to you, by this kind tender of your love; and I am sorry to remember that I was ever so rude, to neglect a friend of your importance.—Bring me shoes and a cloak here.—I was going to bed, if you had not come. What tavern is it?

MACI. The Mitre, sir.

DELI. O! Why, Fido! my shoes.—Good faith, it cannot but please her exceedingly.

ENTER FALLACE. FAL. Come, I marle what piece of night-work you have in hand now, that you call for a cloak, and your shoes: What, is this your pander?

DELI. O, sweet wife, speak lower, I would not he should hear thee for a world—

FAL. Hang him, rascal, I cannot abide him for his treachery, with his wild quick-set beard there. Whither go you now with him?

164

DELI. No, whither with him, dear wife; I go alone to a place, from whence I will return instantly.—Good Macilente, acquaint not her with it by any means, it may come so much the more accepted; frame some other answer.—I'll come back immediately.

[EXIT.

FAL. Nay, an I be not worthy to know whither you go, stay till I take knowledge of your coming back.

MACI. Hear you, mistress Deliro.

FAL. So, sir, and what say you?

MACI. Faith, lady, my intents will not deserve this slight respect, when you shall know them.

FAL. Your intents! why, what may your intents be, for God's sake?

MACI. Troth, the time allows no circumstance, lady, therefore know this was but a device to remove your husband hence, and bestow him securely, whilst, with more conveniency, I might report to you a misfortune that hath happened to monsieur Brisk—Nay, comfort, sweet lady. This night, being at supper, a sort of young gallants committed a riot, for the which he only is apprehended and carried to the Counter, where, if your husband, and other creditors, should but have knowledge of him, the poor gentleman were undone for ever.

FAL. Ah me! that he were.

MACI. Now, therefore, if you can think upon any present means for his delivery, do not foreslow it. A bribe to the officer that committed him will do it.

FAL. O lord, sir! he shall not want for a bribe; pray you, will you commend me to him, and say I'll visit him presently.

MACI. No, lady, I shall do you better service, in protracting your husband's return, that you may go with more safety.

FAL. Good truth, so you may; farewell, good sir.

[EXIT MACI.]—Lord, how a woman may be mistaken in a man! I would have sworn upon all the Testaments in the world he had not loved master Brisk. Bring me my keys there, maid. Alas, good gentleman, if all I have in this earthly world will pleasure him, it shall be at his service.

[EXIT.

MIT. How Macilente sweats in this business, if you mark him!

COR. Ay, you shall see the true picture of spite, anon: here comes the pawn and his redeemer.

SCENE VI.—A ROOM AT THE MITRE.

ENTER DELIRO, FUNGOSO, AND GEORGE.

DELI. Come, brother, be not discouraged for this, man; what!

FUNG. No, truly, I am not discouraged; but I protest to you, brother, I have done imitating any more gallants either in purse or apparel, but as shall become a gentleman, for good carriage, or so.

DELI. You say well.—This is all in the bill here, is it not?

GEORGE. Ay, sir.

DELI. There's your money, tell it: and, brother, I am glad I met with so good occasion to shew my love to you.

FUNG. I will study to deserve it in good truth an I live.

DELI. What, is it right?

GEORGE. Ay, sir, and I thank you.

FUNG. Let me have a capon's leg saved, now the reckoning is paid.

GEORGE. You shall, sir

[EXIT.

ENTER MACILENTE. MACI. Where's signior Deliro?

DELI. Here, Macilente.

MACI. Hark you, sir, have you dispatch'd this same?

DELI. Ay, marry have I.

MACI. Well then, I can tell you news; Brisk is in the Counter.

DELI. In the Counter!

MACI. 'Tis true, sir, committed for the stir here tonight. Now would I
    have you send your brother home afore him, with the report of
    this your kindness done him, to his sister, which will so pleasingly
    possess her, and out of his mouth too, that in the meantime you
    may clap your action on Brisk, and your wife, being in so happy
    a mood, cannot entertain it ill, by any means.
DELI. 'Tis very true, she cannot, indeed, I think.
MACI. Think! why 'tis past thought; you shall never meet the like
    opportunity, I assure you.
DELI. I will do it.—Brother, pray you go home afore (this gentleman
    and I have some private business), and tell my sweet wife I'll
    come presently.
FUNG. I will, brother.
MACI. And, signior, acquaint your sister, how liberally, and out of
    his bounty, your brother has used you (do you see?), made you
    a man of good reckoning; redeem'd that you never were possest
    of, credit; gave you as gentlemanlike terms as might be; found
    no fault with your coming behind the fashion; nor nothing.
FUNG. Nay, I am out of those humours now.
MACI. Well, if you be out, keep your distance, and be not made a shot-
    clog any more.—Come, signior, let's make haste. [EXEUNT.

SCENE VII.—THE COUNTER.

ENTER FALLACE AND FASTIDIOUS BRISK.

FAL. O, master Fastidious, what pity is it to see so sweet a man as you
    are, in so sour a place! [KISSES HIM.
COR. As upon her lips, does she mean?
MIT. O, this is to be imagined the Counter, belike.

FAST. Troth, fair lady, 'tis first the pleasure of the fates, and next of the constable, to have it so: but I am patient, and indeed comforted the more in your kind visit.

FAL. Nay, you shall be comforted in me more than this, if you please, sir. I sent you word by my brother, sir, that my husband laid to 'rest you this morning; I know now whether you received it or no.

FAST. No, believe it, sweet creature, your brother gave me no such intelligence.

FAL. O, the lord!

FAST. But has your husband any such purpose?

FAL. O, sweet master Brisk, yes: and therefore be presently discharged, for if he come with his actions upon you, Lord deliver you! you are in for one half-a-score year; he kept a poor man in Ludgate once twelve year for sixteen shillings. Where's your keeper? for love's sake call him, let him take a bribe, and despatch you. Lord, how my heart trembles! here are no spies, are there?

FAST. No, sweet mistress. Why are you in this passion?

FAL. O lord, master Fastidious, if you knew how I took up my husband today, when he said he would arrest you; and how I railed at him that persuaded him to it, the scholar there (who, on my conscience, loves you now), and what care I took to send you intelligence by my brother; and how I gave him four sovereigns for his pains: and now, how I came running out hither without man or boy with me, so soon as I heard on't; you'd say I were in a passion indeed. Your keeper, for God's sake! O, master Brisk, as 'tis in 'Euphues', 'Hard is the choice, when one is compelled either by silence to die with grief, or by speaking to live with shame'.

FAST. Fair lady, I conceive you, and may this kiss assure you, that where adversity hath, as it were, contracted, prosperity shall not—Od's me! your husband.

ENTER DELIRO AND MACILENTE. FAL. O me!

DELI. Ay! Is it thus?

168

MACI. Why, how now, signior Deliro! has the wolf seen you, ha? Hath Gorgon's head made marble of you?

DELI. Some planet strike me dead!

MACI. Why, look you, sir, I told you, you might have suspected this long afore, had you pleased, and have saved this labour of admiration now, and passion, and such extremities as this frail lump of flesh is subject unto. Nay, why do you not doat now, signior? methinks you should say it were some enchantment, 'deceptio visus', or so, ha! If you could persuade yourself it were a dream now, 'twere excellent: faith, try what you can do, signior: it may be your imagination will be brought to it in time; there's nothing impossible.

FAL. Sweet husband!

DELI. Out, lascivious strumpet!

[EXIT.

MACI. What! did you see how ill that stale vein became him afore, of 'sweet wife', and 'dear heart'; and are you fallen just into the same now, with 'sweet husband'! Away, follow him, go, keep state: what! remember you are a woman, turn impudent; give him not the head, though you give him the horns. Away. And yet, methinks, you should take your leave of 'enfant perdu' here, your forlorn hope.

[EXIT FAL.]—How now, monsieur Brisk? what! Friday night, and in affliction too, and yet your pulpamenta, your delicate morsels! I perceive the affection of ladies and gentlewomen pursues you wheresoever you go, monsieur.

FAST. Now, in good faith, and as I am gentle, there could not have come a thing in this world to have distracted me more, than the wrinkled fortunes of this poor dame.

MACI. O yes, sir; I can tell you a think will distract you much better, believe it: Signior Deliro has entered three actions against you, three actions, monsieur! marry, one of them (I'll put you in comfort) is but three thousand, and the other two, some five thousand pound together: trifles, trifles.

169

FAST. O, I am undone.

MACI. Nay, not altogether so, sir; the knight must have his hundred pound repaid, that will help too; and then six score pounds for a diamond, you know where. These be things will weigh, monsieur, they will weigh.

FAST. O heaven!

MACI. What! do you sigh? this is to 'kiss the hand of a countess', to 'have her coach sent for you', to 'hang poniards in ladies' garters', to 'wear bracelets of their hair', and for every one of these great favours to 'give some slight jewel of five hundred crowns, or so'; why, 'tis nothing. Now, monsieur, you see the plague that treads on the heels o' your foppery: well, go your ways in, remove yourself to the two-penny ward quickly, to save charges, and there set up your rest to spend sir Puntarvolo's hundred pound for him. Away, good pomander, go!

           [EXIT FASTIDIOUS.

Why here's a change! now is my soul at peace:
I am as empty of all envy now,
As they of merit to be envied at.
My humour, like a flame, no longer lasts
Than it hath stuff to feed it; and their folly
Being now raked up in their repentant ashes,
Affords no ampler subject to my spleen.
I am so far from malicing their states,
That I begin to pity them. It grieves me
To think they have a being. I could wish
They might turn wise upon it, and be saved now,
So heaven were pleased; but let them vanish, vapours!—
Gentlemen, how like you it? has't not been tedious?

COR. Nay, we have done censuring now.

MIT. Yes, faith.

MACI. How so?

COR. Marry, because we'll imitate your actors, and be out of our humours. Besides, here are those round about you of more ability in censure than we, whose judgments can give it a more satisfying allowance; we'll refer you to them. [EXEUNT CORDATUS AND MITIS.

MACI. [COMING FORWARD.] Ay, is it even so?—Well, gentlemen, I should have gone in, and return'd to you as I was Asper at the first; but by reason the shift would have been somewhat long, and we are loth to draw your patience farther, we'll entreat you to imagine it. And now, that you may see I will be out of humour for company, I stand wholly to your kind approbation, and indeed am nothing so peremptory as I was in the beginning: marry, I will not do as Plautus in his 'Amphytrio', for all this, 'summi Jovis causa plaudite'; beg a plaudite for God's sake; but if you, out of the bounty of your good-liking, will bestow it, why, you may in time make lean Macilente as fat as sir John Falstaff.

      [EXIT.

THE EPILOGUE

AT THE PRESENTATION BEFORE
QUEEN ELIZABETH

BY MACILENTE.

Never till now did object greet mine eyes
With any light content: but in her graces
All my malicious powers have lost their stings.
Envy is fled from my soul at sight of her,
And she hath chased all black thoughts from my bosom,
Like as the sun doth darkness from the world,
My stream of humour is run out of me,
And as our city's torrent, bent t'infect
The hallow'd bowels of the silver Thames,
Is check'd by strength and clearness of the river,
Till it hath spent itself even at the shore;
So in the ample and unmeasured flood
Of her perfections, are my passions drown'd;
And I have now a spirit as sweet and clear
As the more rarefied and subtle air:—
With which, and with a heart as pure as fire,
Yet humble as the earth, do I implore
[KNEELS.
O heaven, that She, whose presence hath effected

This change in me, may suffer most late change
In her admired and happy government:
May still this Island be call'd Fortunate,
And rugged Treason tremble at the sound,
When Fame shall speak it with an emphasis.
Let foreign polity be dull as lead,
And pale Invasion come with half a heart,
When he but looks upon her blessed soil.
The throat of War be stopt within her land,
And turtle-footed Peace dance fairy rings
About her court; where never may there come
Suspect or danger, but all trust and safety.
Let Flattery be dumb, and Envy blind
In her dread presence; Death himself admire her;
And may her virtues make him to forget
The use of his inevitable hand.
Fly from her, Age; sleep, Time, before her throne;
Our strongest wall falls down, when she is gone.

GLOSSARY

ABATE, cast down, subdue

ABHORRING, repugnant (to), at variance

ABJECT, base, degraded thing, outcast

ABRASE, smooth, blank

ABSOLUTE(LY), faultless(ly)

ABSTRACTED, abstract, abstruse

ABUSE, deceive, insult, dishonour, make ill use of

ACATER, caterer

ACATES, cates

ACCEPTIVE, willing, ready to accept, receive

ACCOMMODATE, fit, befitting. (The word was a fashionable one and used on all occasions. See "Henry IV.," pt. 2, iii.4)

ACCOST, draw near, approach

ACKNOWN, confessedly acquainted with

ACME, full maturity

ADALANTADO, lord deputy or governor of a Spanish province

ADJECTION, addition

ADMIRATION, astonishment

ADMIRE, wonder, wonder at

ADROP, philosopher's stone, or substance from which obtained

ADSCRIVE, subscribe

ADULTERATE, spurious, counterfeit

ADVANCE, life

ADVERTISE, inform, give intelligence

ADVERTISED, "be—," be it known to you

ADVERTISEMENT, intelligence

ADVISE, consider, bethink oneself, deliberate

ADVISED, informed, aware; "are you—?" have you found that out?

AFFECT, love, like; aim at; move

AFFECTED, disposed; beloved

AFFECTIONATE, obstinate; prejudiced

AFFECTS, affections

AFFRONT, "give the—," face

AFFY, have confidence in; betroth

AFTER, after the manner of

AGAIN, AGAINST, in anticipation of

AGGRAVATE, increase, magnify, enlarge upon

AGNOMINATION. See Paranomasie

AIERY, nest, brood

AIM, guess

ALL HID, children's cry at hide-and-seek

ALL-TO, completely, entirely ("all-to-be-laden")

ALLOWANCE, approbation, recognition

ALMA-CANTARAS (astron.), parallels of altitude

ALMAIN, name of a dance

ALMUTEN, planet of chief influence in the horoscope

ALONE, unequalled, without peer

ALUDELS, subliming pots

AMAZED, confused, perplexed

AMBER, AMBRE, ambergris

AMBREE, MARY, a woman noted for her valour at the siege of Ghent, 1458

AMES-ACE, lowest throw at dice

AMPHIBOLIES, ambiguities

AMUSED, bewildered, amazed

AN, if

ANATOMY, skeleton, or dissected body

ANDIRONS, fire-dogs

ANGEL, gold coin worth 10s., stamped with the figure of the archangel Michael

ANNESH CLEARE, spring known as Agnes le Clare

ANSWER, return hit in fencing

ANTIC, ANTIQUE, clown, buffoon

ANTIC, like a buffoon

ANTIPERISTASIS, an opposition which enhances the quality it opposes

APOZEM, decoction

AFFERIL, peril

APPLE-JOHN, APPLE-SQUIRE, pimp, pander

APPLY, attach

APPREHEND, take into custody

APPREHENSIVE, quick of perception; able to perceive and appreciate

APPROVE, prove, confirm

APT, suit, adapt; train, prepare; dispose, incline

APT(LY), suitable(y), opportune(ly)

APTITUDE, suitableness

ARBOR, "make the—," cut up the game (Gifford)

ARCHES, Court of Arches

ARCHIE, Archibald Armstrong, jester to James I. and Charles I.

ARGAILE, argol, crust or sediment in wine casks

ARGENT-VIVE, quicksilver

ARGUMENT, plot of a drama; theme, subject; matter in question; token, proof

ARRIDE, please

ARSEDINE, mixture of copper and zinc, used as an imitation of gold-leaf

ARTHUR, PRINCE, reference to an archery show by a society who assumed arms, etc., of Arthur's knights

ARTICLE, item

ARTIFICIALLY, artfully

ASCENSION, evaporation, distillation

ASPIRE, try to reach, obtain, long for

ASSALTO (Ital.), assault

ASSAY, draw a knife along the belly of the deer, a ceremony of the hunting-field

ASSOIL, solve

ASSURE, secure possession or reversion of

ATHANOR, a digesting furnace, calculated to keep up a constant heat

ATONE, reconcile

ATTACH, attack, seize

AUDACIOUS, having spirit and confidence

AUTHENTIC(AL), of authority, authorised, trustworthy, genuine

AVISEMENT, reflection, consideration

AVOID, begone! get rid of

AWAY WITH, endure

AZOCH, Mercurius Philosophorum

BABION, baboon

BABY, doll

BACK-SIDE, back premises

BAFFLE, treat with contempt

BAGATINE, Italian coin, worth about the third of a farthing

BALARD, horse of magic powers known to old romance

BALDRICK, belt worn across the breast to support bugle, etc.

BALE (of dice), pair

BALK, overlook, pass by, avoid

BALLACE, ballast

BALLOO, game at ball

BALNEUM (BAIN MARIE), a vessel for holding hot water in which other vessels are stood for heating

BANBURY, "brother of _," Puritan

BANDOG, dog tied or chained up

BANE, woe, ruin

BANQUET, a light repast; dessert

BARB, to clip gold

BARBEL, fresh-water fish

BARE, meer; bareheaded; it was "a particular mark of state and grandeur
    for the coachman to be uncovered" (Gifford)

BARLEY-GREAK, game somewhat similar to base

BASE, game of prisoner's base

BASES, richly embroidered skirt reaching to the knees, or lower

BASILISK, fabulous reptile, believed to slay with its eye

BASKET, used for the broken provision collected for prisoners

BASON, basons, etc., were beaten by the attendant mob when bad
    characters were "carted"

BATE, be reduced; abate, reduce

BATOON, baton, stick

BATTEN, feed, grow fat

BAWSON, badger

BEADSMAN, PRAYER-MAN, one engaged to pray for another

BEAGLE, small hound; fig. spy

BEAR IN HAND, keep in suspense, deceive with false hopes

BEARWARD, bear leader

BEDPHERE See Phere

BEDSTAFF, (?) wooden pin in the side of the bedstead for supporting
    the bedclothes (Johnson); one of the sticks of "laths"; a stick used
    in making a bed

BEETLE, heavy mallet

BEG, "I'd—him," the custody of minors and idiots was begged for;
    likewise property fallen forfeit to the Crown ("your house had been
    begged")

BELL-MAN, night watchman

BENJAMIN, an aromatic gum

BERLINA, pillory

BESCUMBER, defile

BESLAVE, beslabber

BESOGNO, beggar

BESPAWLE, bespatter

BETHLEHEM GABOR, Transylvanian hero, proclaimed King of Hungary

BEVER, drinking

BEVIS, SIR, knight of romance whose horse was equally celebrated

BEWAY, reveal, make known

BEZANT, heraldic term: small gold circle

BEZOAR'S STONE, a remedy known by this name was a supposed antidote to poison

BID-STAND, highwayman

BIGGIN, cap, similar to that worn by the Beguines; nightcap

BILIVE (belive), with haste

BILE, nothing, empty talk

BILL, kind of pike

BILLET, wood cut for fuel, stick

BIRDING, thieving

BLACK SANCTUS, burlesque hymn, any unholy riot

BLANK, originally a small French coin

BLANK, white

BLANKET, toss in a blanket

BLAZE, outburst of violence

BLAZE, (her.) blazon; publish abroad

BLAZON, armorial bearings; fig. all that pertains to good birth and breeding

BLIN, "withouten—," without ceasing

BLOW, puff up

BLUE, colour of servants' livery, hence "—order," "—waiters"

180

BLUSHET, blushing one

BOB, jest, taunt

BOB, beat, thump

BODGE, measure

BODKIN, dagger, or other short, pointed weapon; long pin with which the women fastened up their hair

BOLT, roll (of material)

BOLT, dislodge, rout out; sift (boulting-tub)

BOLT'S-HEAD, long, straight-necked vessel for distillation.

BOMBARD SLOPS, padded, puffed-out breeches

BONA ROBA, "good, wholesome, plum-cheeked wench" (Johnson)—not always used in compliment

BONNY-CLABBER, sour butter-milk

BOOKHOLDER, prompter

BOOT, "to—," into the bargain; "no—," of no avail

BORACHIO, bottle made of skin

BORDELLO, brothel

BORNE IT, conducted, carried it through

BOTTLE (of han), bundle, truss

BOTTOM, skein or ball of thread; vessel

BOURD, jest

BOVOLI, snails or cockles dressed in the Italian manner (Gifford)

BOW-POT, flower vase or pot

BOYE, "terrible—," "angry—," roystering young bucks. (See Nares)

BRABBLES (BRABBLESH), brawls

BRACH, bitch

BRADAMANTE, a heroine in 'Orlando Furioso'

BRADLEY, ARTHUR OF, a lively character commemorated in ballads

BRAKE, frame for confining a norse's feet while being shod, or strong curb or bridle; trap

BRANCHED, with "detached sleeve ornaments, projecting from the shoulders of the gown" (Gifford)

BRANDISH, flourish of weapon
BRASH, brace
BRAVE, bravado, braggart speech
BRAVE (adv.), gaily, finely (apparelled)
BRAVERIES, gallants
BRAVERY, extravagant gaiety of apparel
BRAVO, bravado, swaggerer
BRAZEN-HEAD, speaking head made by Roger Bacon
BREATHE, pause for relaxation; exercise
BREATH UPON, speak dispraisingly of
BREND, burn
BRIDE-ALE, wedding feast
BRIEF, abstract; (mus.) breve
BRISK, smartly dressed
BRIZE, breese, gadfly
BROAD-SEAL, state seal
BROCK, badger (term of contempt)
BROKE, transact business as a broker
BROOK, endure, put up with
BROUGHTON, HUGH, an English divine and Hebrew scholar
BRUIT, rumour
BUCK, wash
BUCKLE, bend
BUFF, leather made of buffalo skin, used for military and serjeants' coats, etc.
BUFO, black tincture
BUGLE, long-shaped bead
BULLED, (?) boiled, swelled
BULLIONS, trunk hose
BULLY, term of familiar endearment
BUNGY, Friar Bungay, who had a familiar in the shape of a dog
BURDEN, refrain, chorus

182

BURGONET, closely-fitting helmet with visor

BURGULLION, braggadocio

BURN, mark wooden measures ("—ing of cans")

BURROUGH, pledge, security

BUSKIN, half-boot, foot gear reaching high up the leg

BUTT-SHAFT, barbless arrow for shooting at butts

BUTTER, NATHANIEL. ("Staple of News"), a compiler of general news. (See Cunningham)

BUTTERY-HATCH, half-door shutting off the buttery, where provisions and liquors were stored

BUY, "he bought me," formerly the guardianship of wards could be bought

BUZ, exclamation to enjoin silence

BUZZARD, simpleton

BY AND BY, at once

BY(E), "on the _," incidentally, as of minor or secondary importance; at the side

BY-CHOP, by-blow, bastard

CADUCEUS, Mercury's wand

CALIVER, light kind of musket

CALLET, woman of ill repute

CALLOT, coif worn on the wigs of our judges or serjeants-at-law (Gifford)

CALVERED, crimped, or sliced and pickled. (See Nares)

CAMOUCCIO, wretch, knave

CAMUSED, flat

CAN, knows

CANDLE-RENT, rent from house property

CANDLE-WASTER, one who studies late

CANTER, sturdy beggar

CAP OF MAINTENCE, an insignia of dignity, a cap of state borne before kings at their coronation; also an heraldic term

CAPABLE, able to comprehend, fit to receive instruction, impression

CAPANEUS, one of the "Seven against Thebes"

CARACT, carat, unit of weight for precious stones, etc.; value, worth

CARANZA, Spanish author of a book on duelling

CARCANET, jewelled ornament for the neck

CARE, take care; object

CAROSH, coach, carriage

CARPET, table-cover

CARRIAGE, bearing, behaviour

CARWHITCHET, quip, pun

CASAMATE, casemate, fortress

CASE, a pair

CASE, "in—," in condition

CASSOCK, soldier's loose overcoat

CAST, flight of hawks, couple

CAST, throw dice; vomit; forecast, calculate

CAST, cashiered

CASTING-GLASS, bottle for sprinkling perfume

CASTRIL, kestrel, falcon

CAT, structure used in sieges

CATAMITE, old form of "ganymede"

CATASTROPHE, conclusion

CATCHPOLE, sheriff's officer

CATES, dainties, provisions

CATSO, rogue, cheat

CAUTELOUS, crafty, artful

CENSURE, criticism; sentence

CENSURE, criticise; pass sentence, doom

CERUSE, cosmetic containing white lead

CESS, assess

CHANGE, "hunt—," follow a fresh scent

CHAPMAN, retail dealer

CHARACTER, handwriting

CHARGE, expense

CHARM, subdue with magic, lay a spell on, silence

CHARMING, exercising magic power

CHARTEL, challenge

CHEAP, bargain, market

CHEAR, CHEER, comfort, encouragement; food, entertainment

CHECK AT, aim reproof at

CHEQUIN, gold Italian coin

CHEVEIL, from kidskin, which is elastic and pliable

CHIAUS, Turkish envoy; used for a cheat, swindler

CHILDERMASS DAY, Innocents' Day

CHOKE-BAIL, action which does not allow of bail

CHRYSOPOEIA, alchemy

CHRYSOSPERM, ways of producing gold

CIBATION, adding fresh substances to supply the waste of evaporation

CIMICI, bugs

CINOPER, cinnabar

CIOPPINI, chopine, lady's high shoe

CIRCLING BOY, "a species of roarer; one who in some way drew a man into a snare, to cheat or rob him" (Nares)

CIRCUMSTANCE, circumlocution, beating about the bush; ceremony, everything pertaining to a certain condition; detail, particular

CITRONISE, turn citron colour

CITTERN, kind of guitar

CITY-WIRES, woman of fashion, who made use of wires for hair and dress

CIVIL, legal

CLAP, clack, chatter

CLAPPER-DUDGEON, downright beggar

CLAPS HIS DISH, a clap, or clack, dish (dish with a movable lid) was carried by beggars and lepers to show that the vessel was empty, and to give sound of their approach

CLARIDIANA, heroine of an old romance

CLARISSIMO, Venetian noble

CLEM, starve

CLICKET, latch

CLIM O' THE CLOUGHS, etc., wordy heroes of romance

CLIMATE, country

CLOSE, secret, private; secretive

CLOSENESS, secrecy

CLOTH, arras, hangings

CLOUT, mark shot at, bull's eye

CLOWN, countryman, clodhopper

COACH-LEAVES, folding blinds

COALS, "bear no—," submit to no affront

COAT-ARMOUR, coat of arms

COAT-CARD, court-card

COB-HERRING, HERRING-COB, a young herring

COB-SWAN, male swan

COCK-A-HOOP, denoting unstinted jollity; thought to be derived from turning on the tap that all might drink to the full of the flowing liquor

COCKATRICE, reptile supposed to be produced from a cock's egg and to kill by its eye—used as a term of reproach for a woman

COCK-BRAINED, giddy, wild

COCKER, pamper

COCKSCOMB, fool's cap

COCKSTONE, stone said to be found in a cock's gizzard, and to possess particular virtues

CODLING, softening by boiling

COFFIN, raised crust of a pie

COG, cheat, wheedle

COIL, turmoil, confusion, ado

COKELY, master of a puppet-show (Whalley)

COKES, fool, gull

COLD-CONCEITED, having cold opinion of, coldly affected towards

COLE-HARBOUR, a retreat for people of all sorts

COLLECTION, composure; deduction

COLLOP, small slice, piece of flesh

COLLY, blacken

COLOUR, pretext

COLOURS, "fear no——," no enemy (quibble)

COLSTAFF, cowlstaff, pole for carrying a cowl=tub

COME ABOUT, charge, turn round

COMFORTABLE BREAD, spiced gingerbread

COMING, forward, ready to respond, complaisant

COMMENT, commentary; "sometime it is taken for a lie or fayned tale" (Bullokar, 1616)

COMMODITY, "current for——," allusion to practice of money-lenders, who forced the borrower to take part of the loan in the shape of worthless goods on which the latter had to make money if he could

COMMUNICATE, share

COMPASS, "in——," within the range, sphere

COMPLEMENT, completion, completement; anything required for the perfecting or carrying out of a person or affair; accomplishment

COMPLEXION, natural disposition, constitution

COMPLIMENT, See Complement

COMPLIMENTARIES, masters of accomplishments

COMPOSITION, constitution; agreement, contract

COMPOSURE, composition

COMPTER, COUNTER, debtors' prison

CONCEALMENT, a certain amount of church property had been retained at the dissolution of the monasteries; Elizabeth sent commissioners to search it out, and the courtiers begged for it

CONCEIT, idea, fancy, witty invention, conception, opinion

CONCEIT, apprehend

CONCEITED, fancifully, ingeniously devised or conceived; possessed of intelligence, witty, ingenious (hence well conceited, etc.); disposed to joke; of opinion, possessed of an idea

CONCEIVE, understand

CONCENT, harmony, agreement

CONCLUDE, infer, prove

CONCOCT, assimilate, digest

CONDEN'T, probably conducted

CONDUCT, escort, conductor

CONEY-CATCH, cheat

CONFECT, sweetmeat

CONFER, compare

CONGIES, bows

CONNIVE, give a look, wink, of secret intelligence

CONSORT, company, concert

CONSTANCY, fidelity, ardour, persistence

CONSTANT, confirmed, persistent, faithful

CONSTANTLY, firmly, persistently

CONTEND, strive

CONTINENT, holding together

CONTROL (the point), bear or beat down

CONVENT, assembly, meeting

CONVERT, turn (oneself)

CONVEY, transmit from one to another

CONVINCE, evince, prove; overcome, overpower; convict

COP, head, top; tuft on head of birds; "a cop" may have reference to one or other meaning; Gifford and others interpret as "conical, terminating in a point"

COPE-MAN, chapman

COPESMATE, companion

CORV (Lat. Copia), abundance, copiousness

CORN ("powder-"), grain

COROLLARY, finishing part or touch

CORSIVE, corrosive

CORTINE, curtain, (arch.) wall between two towers, etc.

CORYAT, famous for his travels, published as 'Coryat's Crudities'

COSSET, pet lamb, pet

COSTARD, head

COSTARD-MONGER, apple-seller, coster-monger

COSTS, ribs

COTE, hut

COTHURNAL, from "cothurnus," a particular boot worn by actors in Greek tragedy

COTQUEAN, hussy

COUNSEL, secret

COUNTENANCE, means necessary for support; credit, standing

COUNTER. See Compter

COUNTER, pieces of metal or ivory for calculating at play

COUNTER, "hunt—," follow scent in reverse direction

COUNTERFEIT, false coin

COUNTERPANE, one part or counterpart of a deed or indenture

COUNTERPOINT, opposite, contrary point

COURT-DISH, a kind of drinking-cup (Halliwell); N.E.D. quotes from Bp. Goodman's 'Court of James I.: "The king . . . caused his carver to cut him out a court-dish, that is, something of every dish, which he sent him as part of his reversion," but this does not sound like short allowance or small receptacle

COURT-DOR, fool

COURTEAU, curtal, small horse with docked tail

COURTSHIP, courtliness

COVETISE, avarice

COWSHARD, cow dung

COXCOMB, fool's cap, fool

COY, shrink; disdain

COYSTREL, low varlet

COZEN, cheat

CRACK, lively young rogue, wag

CRACK, crack up, boast; come to grief

CRAMBE, game of crambo, in which the players find rhymes for a given word

CRANCH, craunch

CRANTON, spider-like; also fairy appellation for a fly (Gifford, who refers to lines in Drayton's "Nimphidia")

CRIMP, game at cards

CRINCLE, draw back, turn aside

CRISPED, with curled or waved hair

CROP, gather, reap

CROPSHIRE, a kind of herring. (See N.E.D.)

CROSS, any piece of money, many coins being stamped with a cross

CROSS AND FILE, heads and tails

CROSSLET, crucible

CROWD, fiddle

CRUDITIES, undigested matter

CRUMP, curl up

CRUSADO, Portuguese gold coin, marked with a cross

CRY ("he that cried Italian):, "speak in a musical cadence," intone, or declaim(?); cry up

CUCKING-STOOL, used for the ducking of scolds, etc.

CUCURBITE, a gourd-shaped vessel used for distillation

CUERPO, "in—," in undress
CULLICE, broth
CULLION, base fellow, coward
CULLISEN, badge worn on their arm by servants
CULVERIN, kind of cannon
CUNNING, skill
CUNNING, skilful
CUNNING-MAN, fortune-teller
CURE, care for
CURIOUS(LY), scrupulous, particular; elaborate, elegant(ly), dainty(ly) (hence "in curious")
CURST, shrewish, mischievous
CURTAL, dog with docked tail, of inferior sort
CUSTARD, "quaking—," "—politic," reference to a large custard which formed part of a city feast and afforded huge entertainment, for the fool jumped into it, and other like tricks were played. (See "All's Well, etc." ii. 5, 40)
CUTWORK, embroidery, open-work
CYPRES (CYPRUS) (quibble), cypress (or cyprus) being a transparent material, and when black used for mourning

DAGGER ("—frumety"), name of tavern
DARGISON, apparently some person known in ballad or tale
DAUPHIN MY BOY, refrain of old comic song
DAW, daunt
DEAD LIFT, desperate emergency
DEAR, applied to that which in any way touches us nearly
DECLINE, turn off from; turn away, aside
DEFALK, deduct, abate
DEFEND, forbid
DEGENEROUS, degenerate
DEGREES, steps

DELATE, accuse

DEMI-CULVERIN, cannon carrying a ball of about ten pounds

DENIER, the smallest possible coin, being the twelfth part of a sou

DEPART, part with

DEPENDANCE, ground of quarrel in duello language

DESERT, reward

DESIGNMENT, design

DESPERATE, rash, reckless

DETECT, allow to be detected, betray, inform against

DETERMINE, terminate

DETRACT, draw back, refuse

DEVICE, masque, show; a thing moved by wires, etc., puppet

DEVISE, exact in every particular

DEVISED, invented

DIAPASM, powdered aromatic herbs, made into balls of perfumed
    paste. (See Pomander)

DIBBLE, (?) moustache (N.E.D.); (?) dagger (Cunningham)

DIFFUSED, disordered, scattered, irregular

DIGHT, dressed

DILDO, refrain of popular songs; vague term of low meaning

DIMBLE, dingle, ravine

DIMENSUM, stated allowance

DISBASE, debase

DISCERN, distinguish, show a difference between

DISCHARGE, settle for

DISCIPLINE, reformation; ecclesiastical system

DISCLAIM, renounce all part in

DISCOURSE, process of reasoning, reasoning faculty

DISCOURTSHIP, discourtesy

DISCOVER, betray, reveal; display

DISFAVOUR, disfigure

DISPARGEMENT, legal term supplied to the unfitness in any way of a
    marriage arranged for in the case of wards
DISPENSE WITH, grant dispensation for
DISPLAY, extend
DIS'PLE, discipline, teach by the whip
DISPOSED, inclined to merriment
DISPOSURE, disposal
DISPRISE, depreciate
DISPUNCT, not punctilious
DISQUISITION, search
DISSOLVED, enervated by grief
DISTANCE, (?) proper measure
DISTASTE, offence, cause of offence
DISTASTE, render distasteful
DISTEMPERED, upset, out of humour
DIVISION (mus.), variation, modulation
DOG-BOLT, term of contempt
DOLE, given in dole, charity
DOLE OF FACES, distribution of grimaces
DOOM, verdict, sentence
DOP, dip, low bow
DOR, beetle, buzzing insect, drone, idler
DOR, (?) buzz; "give the—," make a fool of
DOSSER, pannier, basket
DOTES, endowments, qualities
DOTTEREL, plover; gull, fool
DOUBLE, behave deceitfully
DOXY, wench, mistress
DRACHM, Greek silver coin
DRESS, groom, curry
DRESSING, coiffure
DRIFT, intention

DRYFOOT, track by mere scent of foot
DUCKING, punishment for minor offences
DUILL, grieve
DUMPS, melancholy, originally a mournful melody
DURINDANA, Orlando's sword
DWINDLE, shrink away, be overawed

EAN, yean, bring forth young
EASINESS, readiness
EBOLITION, ebullition
EDGE, sword
EECH, eke
EGREGIOUS, eminently excellent
EKE, also, moreover
E-LA, highest note in the scale
EGGS ON THE SPIT, important business on hand
ELF-LOCK, tangled hair, supposed to be the work of elves
EMMET, ant
ENGAGE, involve
ENGHLE. See Ingle
ENGHLE, cajole; fondle
ENGIN(E), device, contrivance; agent; ingenuity, wit
ENGINER, engineer, deviser, plotter
ENGINOUS, crafty, full of devices; witty, ingenious
ENGROSS, monopolise
ENS, an existing thing, a substance
ENSIGNS, tokens, wounds
ENSURE, assure
ENTERTAIN, take into service
ENTREAT, plead
ENTREATY, entertainment
ENTRY, place where a deer has lately passed

194

ENVOY, denouement, conclusion

ENVY, spite, calumny, dislike, odium

EPHEMERIDES, calendars

EQUAL, just, impartial

ERECTION, elevation in esteem

ERINGO, candied root of the sea-holly, formerly used as a sweetmeat and aphrodisiac

ERRANT, arrant

ESSENTIATE, become assimilated

ESTIMATION, esteem

ESTRICH, ostrich

ETHNIC, heathen

EURIPUS, flux and reflux

EVEN, just equable

EVENT, fate, issue

EVENT(ED), issue(d)

EVERT, overturn

EXACUATE, sharpen

EXAMPLESS, without example or parallel

EXCALIBUR, King Arthur's sword

EXEMPLIFY, make an example of

EXEMPT, separate, exclude

EXEQUIES, obsequies

EXHALE, drag out

EXHIBITION, allowance for keep, pocket-money

EXORBITANT, exceeding limits of propriety or law, inordinate

EXORNATION, ornament

EXPECT, wait

EXPLATE, terminate

EXPLICATE, explain, unfold

EXTEMPORAL, extempore, unpremeditated

EXTRACTION, essence

EXTRAORDINARY, employed for a special or temporary purpose

EXTRUDE, expel

EYE, "in—," in view

EYEBRIGHT, (?) a malt liquor in which the herb of this name was infused, or a person who sold the same (Gifford)

EYE-TINGE, least shade or gleam

FACE, appearance

FACES ABOUT, military word of command

FACINOROUS, extremely wicked

FACKINGS, faith

FACT, deed, act, crime

FACTIOUS, seditious, belonging to a party, given to party feeling

FAECES, dregs

FAGIOLI, French beans

FAIN, forced, necessitated

FAITHFUL, believing

FALL, ruff or band turned back on the shoulders; or, veil

FALSIFY, feign (fencing term)

FAME, report

FAMILIAR, attendant spirit

FANTASTICAL, capricious, whimsical

FARCE, stuff

FAR-FET. See Fet

FARTHINGAL, hooped petticoat

FAUCET, tapster

FAULT, lack; loss, break in line of scent; "for—," in default of

FAUTOR, partisan

FAYLES, old table game similar to backgammon

FEAR(ED), affright(ed)

FEAT, activity, operation; deed, action

FEAT, elegant, trim

196

FEE, "in—" by feudal obligation

FEIZE, beat, belabour

FELLOW, term of contempt

FENNEL, emblem of flattery

FERE, companion, fellow

FERN-SEED, supposed to have power of rendering invisible

FET, fetched

FETCH, trick

FEUTERER (Fr. vautrier), dog-keeper

FEWMETS, dung

FICO, fig

FIGGUM, (?) jugglery

FIGMENT, fiction, invention

FIRK, frisk, move suddenly, or in jerks; "—up," stir up, rouse; "firks
    mad," suddenly behaves like a madman

FIT, pay one out, punish

FITNESS, readiness

FITTON (FITTEN), lie, invention

FIVE-AND-FIFTY, "highest number to stand on at primero" (Gifford)

FLAG, to fly low and waveringly

FLAGON CHAIN, for hanging a smelling-bottle (Fr. flacon) round the
    neck (?). (See N.E.D.)

FLAP-DRAGON, game similar to snap-dragon

FLASKET, some kind of basket

FLAW, sudden gust or squall of wind

FLAWN, custard

FLEA, catch fleas

FLEER, sneer, laugh derisively

FLESH, feed a hawk or dog with flesh to incite it to the chase; initiate in
    blood-shed; satiate

FLICKER-MOUSE, bat

FLIGHT, light arrow

FLITTER-MOUSE, bat

FLOUT, mock, speak and act contemptuously

FLOWERS, pulverised substance

FLY, familiar spirit

FOIL, weapon used in fencing; that which sets anything off to advantage

FOIST, cut-purse, sharper

FOND(LY), foolish(ly)

FOOT-CLOTH, housings of ornamental cloth which hung down on either side a horse to the ground

FOOTING, foothold; footstep; dancing

FOPPERY, foolery

FOR, "—failing," for fear of failing

FORBEAR, bear with; abstain from

FORCE, "hunt at—," run the game down with dogs

FOREHEAD, modesty; face, assurance, effrontery

FORESLOW, delay

FORESPEAK, bewitch; foretell

FORETOP, front lock of hair which fashion required to be worn upright

FORGED, fabricated

FORM, state formally

FORMAL, shapely; normal; conventional

FORTHCOMING, produced when required

FOUNDER, disable with over-riding

FOURM, form, lair

FOX, sword

FRAIL, rush basket in which figs or raisins were packed

FRAMFULL, peevish, sour-tempered

FRAPLER, blusterer, wrangler

FRAYING, "a stag is said to fray his head when he rubs it against a tree to . . . cause the outward coat of the new horns to fall off" (Gifford)

FREIGHT (of the gazetti), burden (of the newspapers)

198

FREQUENT, full

FRICACE, rubbing

FRICATRICE, woman of low character

FRIPPERY, old clothes shop

FROCK, smock-frock

FROLICS, (?) humorous verses circulated at least (N.E.D.); couplets
    wrapped round sweetmeats (Cunningham)

FRONTLESS, shameless

FROTED, rubbed

FRUMETY, hulled wheat boiled in milk and spiced

FRUMP, flout, sneer

FUCUS, dye

FUGEAND, (?) figment: flighty, restless (N.E.D.)

FULLAM, false dice

FULMART, polecat

FULSOME, foul, offensive

FURIBUND, raging, furious

GALLEY-FOIST, city-barge, used on Lord Mayor's Day, when he was
    sworn into his office at Westminster (Whalley)

GALLIARD, lively dance in triple time

GAPE, be eager after

GARAGANTUA, Rabelais' giant

GARB, sheaf (Fr. Gerbe); manner, fashion, behaviour

BARD, guard, trimming, gold or silver lace, or other ornament

GARDED, faced or trimmed

GARNISH, fee

GAVEL-KIND, name of a land-tenure existing chiefly in Kent; from
    16th century often used to denote custom of dividing a deceased
    man's property equally among his sons (N.E.D.)

GAZETTE, small Venetian coin worth about three-farthings

GEANCE, jaunt, errand

GEAR (GEER), stuff, matter, affair

GELID, frozen

GEMONIES, steps from which the bodies of criminals were thrown into the river

GENERAL, free, affable

GENIUS, attendant spirit

GENTRY, gentlemen; manners characteristic of gentry, good breeding

GIB-CAT, tom-cat

GIGANTOMACHIZE, start a giants' war

GIGLOT, wanton

GIMBLET, gimlet

GING, gang

GLASS ("taking in of shadows, etc."), crystal or beryl

GLEEK, card game played by three; party of three, trio; side glance

GLICK (GLEEK), jest, gibe

GLIDDER, glaze

GLORIOUSLY, of vain glory

GODWIT, bird of the snipe family

GOLD-END-MAN, a buyer of broken gold and silver

GOLL, hand

GONFALIONIER, standard-bearer, chief magistrate, etc.

GOOD, sound in credit

GOOD-Year, good luck

GOOSE-TURD, colour of. (See Turd)

GORCROW, carrion crow

GORGET, neck armour

GOSSIP, godfather

GOWKED, from "gowk," to stand staring and gaping like a fool

GRANNAM, grandam

GRASS, (?) grease, fat

GRATEFUL, agreeable, welcome

GRATIFY, give thanks to

GRATITUDE, gratuity

GRATULATE, welcome, congratulate

GRAVITY, dignity

GRAY, badger

GRICE, cub

GRIEF, grievance

GRIPE, vulture, griffin

GRIPE'S EGG, vessel in shape of

GROAT, fourpence

GROGRAN, coarse stuff made of silk and mohair, or of coarse silk

GROOM-PORTER, officer in the royal household

GROPE, handle, probe

GROUND, pit (hence "grounded judgments")

GUARD, caution, heed

GUARDANT, heraldic term: turning the head only

GUILDER, Dutch coin worth about 4d.

GULES, gullet, throat; heraldic term for red

GULL, simpleton, dupe

GUST, taste

HAB NAB, by, on, chance

HABERGEON, coat of mail

HAGGARD, wild female hawk; hence coy, wild

HALBERD, combination of lance and battle-axe

HALL, "a—!" a cry to clear the room for the dancers

HANDSEL, first money taken

HANGER, loop or strap on a sword-belt from which the sword was suspended

HAP, fortune, luck

HAPPILY, haply

HAPPINESS, appropriateness, fitness

HAPPY, rich

HARBOUR, track, trace (an animal) to its shelter

HARD-FAVOURED, harsh-featured

HARPOCRATES, Horus the child, son of Osiris, figured with a finger pointing to his mouth, indicative of silence

HARRINGTON, a patent was granted to Lord H. for the coinage of tokens (q.v.)

HARROT, herald

HARRY NICHOLAS, founder of a community called the "Family of Love"

HAY, net for catching rabbits, etc.

HAY! (Ital. hai!), you have it (a fencing term)

HAY IN HIS HORN, ill-tempered person

HAZARD, game at dice; that which is staked

HEAD, "first—," young deer with antlers first sprouting; fig. a newly-ennobled man

HEADBOROUGH, constable

HEARKEN AFTER, inquire; "hearken out," find, search out

HEARTEN, encourage

HEAVEN AND HELL ("Alchemist"), names of taverns

HECTIC, fever

HEDGE IN, include

HELM, upper part of a retort

HER'NSEW, hernshaw, heron

HIERONIMO (JERONIMO), hero of Kyd's "Spanish Tragedy"

HOBBY, nag

HOBBY-HORSE, imitation horse of some light material, fastened round the waist of the morrice-dancer, who imitated the movements of a skittish horse

HODDY-DODDY, fool

HOIDEN, hoyden, formerly applied to both sexes (ancient term for leveret? Gifford)

HOLLAND, name of two famous chemists

HONE AND HONERO, wailing expressions of lament or discontent

HOOD-WIND'D, blindfolded

HORARY, hourly

HORN-MAD, stark mad (quibble)

HORN-THUMB, cut-purses were in the habit of wearing a horn shield on the thumb

HORSE-BREAD-EATING, horses were often fed on coarse bread

HORSE-COURSES, horse-dealer

HOSPITAL, Christ's Hospital

HOWLEGLAS, Eulenspiegel, the hero of a popular German tale which related his buffooneries and knavish tricks

HUFF, hectoring, arrogance

HUFF IT, swagger

HUISHER (Fr. huissier), usher

HUM, beer and spirits mixed together

HUMANITIAN, humanist, scholar

HUMOROUS, capricious, moody, out of humour; moist

HUMOUR, a word used in and out of season in the time of Shakespeare and Ben Jonson, and ridiculed by both

HUMOURS, manners

HUMPHREY, DUKE, those who were dinnerless spent the dinner-hour in a part of St. Paul's where stood a monument said to be that of the duke's; hence "dine with Duke Humphrey," to go hungry

HURTLESS, harmless

IDLE, useless, unprofitable

ILL-AFFECTED, ill-disposed

ILL-HABITED, unhealthy

ILLUSTRATE, illuminate

IMBIBITION, saturation, steeping

IMBROCATA, fencing term: a thrust in tierce

IMPAIR, impairment

IMPART, give money

IMPARTER, any one ready to be cheated and to part with his money

IMPEACH, damage

IMPERTINENCIES, irrelevancies

IMPERTINENT(LY), irrelevant(ly), without reason or purpose

IMPOSITION, duty imposed by

IMPOTENTLY, beyond power of control

IMPRESS, money in advance

IMPULSION, incitement

IN AND IN, a game played by two or three persons with four dice

INCENSE, incite, stir up

INCERATION, act of covering with wax; or reducing a substance to softness of wax

INCH, "to their—es," according to their stature, capabilities

INCH-PIN, sweet-bread

INCONVENIENCE, inconsistency, absurdity

INCONY, delicate, rare (used as a term of affection)

INCUBEE, incubus

INCUBUS, evil spirit that oppresses us in sleep, nightmare

INCURIOUS, unfastidious, uncritical

INDENT, enter into engagement

INDIFFERENT, tolerable, passable

INDIGESTED, shapeless, chaotic

INDUCE, introduce

INDUE, supply

INEXORABLE, relentless

INFANTED, born, produced

INFLAME, augment charge

INGENIOUS, used indiscriminantly for ingenuous; intelligent, talented

INGENUITY, ingenuousness

INGENUOUS, generous

INGINE. See Engin

204

INGINER, engineer. (See Enginer)

INGLE, OR ENGHLE, bosom friend, intimate, minion

INHABITABLE, uninhabitable

INJURY, insult, affront

IN-MATE, resident, indwelling

INNATE, natural

INNOCENT, simpleton

INQUEST, jury, or other official body of inquiry

INQUISITION, inquiry

INSTANT, immediate

INSTRUMENT, legal document

INSURE, assure

INTEGRATE, complete, perfect

INTELLIGENCE, secret information, news

INTEND, note carefully, attend, give ear to, be occupied with

INTENDMENT, intention

INTENT, intention, wish

INTENTION, concentration of attention or gaze

INTENTIVE, attentive

INTERESSED, implicated

INTRUDE, bring in forcibly or without leave

INVINCIBLY, invisibly

INWARD, intimate

IRPE (uncertain), "a fantastic grimace, or contortion of the body: (Gifford)

JACE, Jack o' the clock, automaton figure that strikes the hour;

Jack-a-lent, puppet thrown at in Lent

JACK, key of a virginal

JACOB'S STAFF, an instrument for taking altitudes and distances

JADE, befool

JEALOUSY, JEALOUS, suspicion, suspicious

JERKING, lashing

JEW'S TRUMP, Jew's harp

JIG, merry ballad or tune; a fanciful dialogue or light comic act introduced at the end or during an interlude of a play

JOINED (JOINT)-STOOL, folding stool

JOLL, jowl

JOLTHEAD, blockhead

JUMP, agree, tally

JUST YEAR, no one was capable of the consulship until he was forty-three

KELL, cocoon

KELLY, an alchemist

KEMB, comb

KEMIA, vessel for distillation

KIBE, chap, sore

KILDERKIN, small barrel

KILL, kiln

KIND, nature; species; "do one's—," act according to one's nature

KIRTLE, woman's gown of jacket and petticoat

KISS OR DRINK AFORE ME, "this is a familiar expression, employed when what the speaker is just about to say is anticipated by another" (Gifford)

KIT, fiddle

KNACK, snap, click

KNIPPER-DOLING, a well-known Anabaptist

KNITTING CUP, marriage cup

KNOCKING, striking, weighty

KNOT, company, band; a sandpiper or robin snipe (Tringa canulus); flower-bed laid out in fanciful design

KURSINED, KYRSIN, christened

LABOURED, wrought with labour and care

LADE, load(ed)

LADING, load

LAID, plotted

LANCE-KNIGHT (Lanzknecht), a German mercenary foot-soldier

LAP, fold

LAR, household god

LARD, garnish

LARGE, abundant

LARUM, alarum, call to arms

LATTICE, tavern windows were furnished with lattices of various colours

LAUNDER, to wash gold in aqua regia, so as imperceptibly to extract some of it.

LAVE, ladle, bale

LAW, "give—," give a start (term of chase)

LAXATIVE, loose

LAY ABOARD, run alongside generally with intent to board

LEAGUER, siege, or camp of besieging army

LEASING, lying

LEAVE, leave off, desist

LEER, leering or "empty, hence, perhaps leer horse without a rider; leer is an adjective meaning uncontrolled, hence 'leer drunkards'" (Halliwell); according to Nares, a leer (empty) horse meant also a led horse; leeward, left

LEESE, lose

LEGS, "make—," do obeisance

LEIGEP, resident representative

LEIGERITY, legerdemain

LEMMA, subject proposed, or title of the epigram

LENTER, slower

LET, hinder

LET, hindrance

LEVEL COIL, a rough game . . . in which one hunted another from his
    seat. Hence used for any noisy riot (Halliwell)

LEWD, ignorant

LEYSTALLS, receptacles of filth

LIBERAL, ample

LIEGER, ledger, register

LIFT(ING), steal(ing)

LIGHT, alight

LIGHTLY, commonly, usually, often

LIKE, please

LIKELY, agreeable, pleasing

LIME-HOUND, leash-, blood-hound

LIMMER, vile, worthless

LIN, leave off

Line, "by—," by rule

LINSTOCK, staff to stick in the ground, with forked head to hold a
    lighted match for firing cannon

LIQUID, clear

LIST, listen, hard; like, please

LIVERY, legal term, delivery of the possession, etc.

LOGGET, small log, stick

LOOSE, solution; upshot, issue; release of an arrow

LOSE, give over, desist from; waste

LOUTING, bowing, cringing

LUCULENT, bright of beauty

LUDGATHIANS, dealers on Ludgate Hill

LURCH, rob, cheat

LUTE, to close a vessel with some kind of cement

MACK, unmeaning expletive

MADGE_HOWLET or own, barn-owl

MAIM, hurt, injury

MAIN, chief concern (used as a quibble on heraldic term for "hand")

MAINPRISE, becoming surety for a prisoner so as to procure his release

MAINTENANCE, giving aid, or abetting

MAKE, mate

MAKE, MADE, acquaint with business, prepare(d), instruct(ed)

MALLANDERS, disease of horses

MALT HORSE, dray horse

MAMMET, puppet

MAMMOTHREPT, spoiled child

MANAGE, control (term used for breaking-in horses); handling, administration

MANGO, slave-dealer

MANGONISE, polish up for sale

MANIPLES, bundles, handfuls

MANKIND, masculine, like a virago

MANEIND, humanity

MAPLE FACE, spotted face (N.E.D.)

MARCH PANE, a confection of almonds, sugar, etc.

MARK, "fly to the——," "generally said of a goshawk when, having 'put in' a covey of partridges, she takes stand, making the spot where they disappeared from view until the falconer arrives to put them out to her" (Harting, Bibl. Accip. Gloss. 226)

MARLE, marvel

MARROW-BONE MAN, one often on his knees for prayer

MARRY! exclamation derived from the Virgin's name

MARRY GIP, "probably originated from By Mary Gipcy = St. Mary of Egypt, (N.E.D.)

MARTAGAN, Turk's cap lily

MARYHINCHCO, stringhalt

MASORETH, Masora, correct form of the scriptural text according to Hebrew tradition

Mass, abb. for master

MAUND, beg

MAUTHER, girl, maid

MEAN, moderation

MEASURE, dance, more especially a stately one

MEAT, "carry—in one's mouth," be a source of money or entertainment

MEATH, metheglin

MECHANICAL, belonging to mechanics, mean, vulgar

MEDITERRANEO, middle aisle of St. Paul's, a general resort for business and amusement

MEET WITH, even with

MELICOTTON, a late kind of peach

MENSTRUE, solvent

MERCAT, market

MERD, excrement

MERE, undiluted; absolute, unmitigated

MESS, party of four

METHEGLIN, fermented liquor, of which one ingredient was honey

METOPOSCOPY, study of physiognomy

MIDDLING GOSSIP, go-between

MIGNIARD, dainty, delicate

MILE-END, training-ground of the city

MINE-MEN, sappers

MINION, form of cannon

MINSITIVE, (?) mincing, affected (N.E.D.)

MISCELLANY MADAM, "a female trader in miscellaneous articles; a dealer in trinkets or ornaments of various kinds, such as kept shops in the New Exchange" (Nares)

MISCELLINE, mixed grain; medley

MISCONCEIT, misconception

MISPRISE, MISPRISION, mistake, misunderstanding

MISTAKE AWAY, carry away as if by mistake

MITHRIDATE, an antidote against poison

MOCCINIGO, small Venetian coin, worth about ninepence

MODERN, in the mode; ordinary, common-place

MOMENT, force or influence of value

MONTANTO, upward stroke

MONTH'S MIND, violent desire

MOORISH, like a moor or waste

MORGLAY, sword of Bevis of Southampton

MORRICe-DANCE, dance on May Day, etc., in which certain personages
    were represented

MORTALITY, death

MORT-MAL, old score, gangrene

MOSCADINO, confection flavoured with musk

MOTHER, Hysterica passio

MOTION, proposal, request; puppet, puppet-show; "one of the small
    figures on the face of a large clock which was moved by the vibration
    of the pendulum" (Whalley)

MOTION, suggest, propose

MOTLEY, parti-coloured dress of a fool; hence used to signify pertaining
    to, or like, a fool

MOTTE, motto

MOURNIVAL, set of four aces or court cards in a hand; a quartette

MOW, setord hay or sheaves of grain

MUCH! expressive of irony and incredulity

MUCKINDER, handkerchief

MULE, "born to ride on—," judges or serjeants-at-law formerly rode on
    mules when going in state to Westminster (Whally)

MULLETS, small pincers

MUM-CHANCE, game of chance, played in silence
MUN, must
MUREY, dark crimson red
MUSCOVY-GLASS, mica
MUSE, wonder
MUSICAL, in harmony
MUSS, mouse; scramble
MYROBOLANE, foreign conserve, "a dried plum, brought from the Indies"
MYSTERY, art, trade, profession.

NAIL, "to the—" (ad unguem), to perfection, to the very utmost
NATIVE, natural
NEAT, cattle
NEAT, smartly apparelled; unmixed; dainty
NEATLY, neatly finished
NEATNESS, elegance
NEIS, nose, scent
NEUF (NEAF, NEIF), fist
NEUFT, newt
NIAISE, foolish, inexperienced person
NICE, fastidious, trivial, finical, scrupulous
NICENESS, fastidiousness
NICK, exact amount; right moment; "set in the—" meaning uncertain
NICE, suit, fit' hit, seize the right moment, etc., exactly hit on, hit off
NOBLE, gold coin worth 6s.8d.
NOCENT, harmful
NIL, not will
NOISE, company of musicians
NOMENTACK, an Indian chief from Virginia
NONES, nonce
NOTABLE, egregious

NOTE, sign, token
NOUGHT, "be—," go to the devil, be hanged, etc.
NOWT-HEAD, blockhead
NUMBER, rhythm
NUPSON, oaf, simpleton

OADE, wood
OBARNI, preparation of mead
OBJECT, oppose; expose; interpose
OBLATRANT, barking, railing
OBNOXIOUS, liable, exposed; offensive
OBSERVANCE, homage, devoted service
OBSERVANT, attentive, obsequious
OBSERVE, show deference, respect
OBSERVER, one who shows deference, or waits upon another
OBSTANCY, legal phrase, "juridical opposition"
OBSTREPEROUS, clamorous, vociferous
OBSTUPEFACT, stupefied
ODLING, (?) "must have some relation to tricking and cheating" (Nares)
OMINOUS, deadly, fatal
ONCE, at once; for good and all; used also for additional emphasis
ONLY, pre-eminent, special
OPEN, make public; expound
OPPILATION, obstruction
OPPONE, oppose
OPPOSITE, antagonist
OFFPRESS, suppress
ORIGINOUS, native
ORT, remnant, scrap
OUT, "to be—." to have forgotten one's part; not at one with each other

OUTCRY, sale by auction

OUTREGUIDANCE, arrogance, presumption

OUTSPEAK, speak more than

OVERPARTED, given too difficult a part to play

OWLSPIEGEL. See Howleglass

OYEZ! (O YES!), hear ye! call of the public crier when about to make a
 proclamation

PACKING PENNY, "give a—," dismiss, send packing

PAD, highway

PAD-HORSE, road-horse

PAINED (PANED) SLOPS, full breeches made of strips of different
 colour and material

PAINFUL, diligent, painstaking

PAINT, blush

PALINODE, ode of recantation

PALL, weaken, dim, make stale

PALM, triumph

PAN, skirt of dress or coat

PANNEL, pad, or rough kind of saddle

PANNIER-ALLY, inhabited by tripe-sellers

PANNIER-MAN, hawker; a man employed about the inns of court to
 bring in provisions, set the table, etc.

PANTOFLE, indoor shoe, slipper

PARAMENTOS, fine trappings

PARANOMASIE, a play upon words

PARANTORY, (?) peremptory

PARCEL, particle, fragment (used contemptuously); article

PARCEL, part, partly

PARCEL-POET, poetaster

PARERGA, subordinate matters

PARGET, to paint or plaster the face

PARLE, parley

PARLOUS, clever, shrewd

PART, apportion

PARTAKE, participate in

PARTED, endowed, talented

PARTICULAR, individual person

PARTIZAN, kind of halberd

PARTRICH, partridge

PARTS, qualities endowments

PASH, dash, smash

PASS, care, trouble oneself

PASSADO, fending term: a thrust

PASSAGE, game at dice

PASSINGLY, exceedingly

PASSION, effect caused by external agency

PASSION, "in—," in so melancholy a tone, so pathetically

PATOUN, (?) Fr. Paton, pellet of dough; perhaps the "moulding of the tobacco ... for the pipe" (Gifford); (?) variant of Petun, South American name of tobacco

PATRICO, the recorder, priest, orator of strolling beggars or gipsies

PATTEN, shoe with wooden sole; "go—," keep step with, accompany

PAUCA VERBA, few words

PAVIN, a stately dance

PEACE, "with my master's—," by leave, favour

PECULIAR, individual, single

PEDANT, teacher of the languages

PEEL, baker's shovel

PEEP, speak in a small or shrill voice

PEEVISH(LY), foolish(ly), capricious(ly); childish(ly)

PELICAN, a retort fitted with tube or tubes, for continuous distillation

PENCIL, small tuft of hair

PERDUE, soldier accustomed to hazardous service

PEREMPTORY, resolute, bold; imperious; thorough, utter, absolute(ly)

PERIMETER, circumference of a figure

PERIOD, limit, end

PERK, perk up

PERPETUANA, "this seems to be that glossy kind of stuff now called everlasting, and anciently worn by serjeants and other city officers" (Gifford)

PERSPICIL, optic glass

PERSTRINGE, criticise, censure

PERSUADE, inculcate, commend

PERSWAY, mitigate

PERTINACY, pertinacity

PESTLING, pounding, pulverising, like a pestle

PETASUS, broad-brimmed hat or winged cap worn by Mercury

PETITIONARY, supplicatory

PETRONEL, a kind of carbine or light gas carried by horsemen

PETULANT, pert, insolent

PHERE. See Fere

PHLEGMA, watery distilled liquor (old chem. "water")

PHRENETIC, madman

PICARDIL, still upright collar fastened on to the coat (Whalley)

PICT-HATCH, disreputable quarter of London

PIECE, person, used for woman or girl; a gold coin worth in Jonson's time 20s. or 22s.

PIECES OF EIGHT, Spanish coin: piastre equal to eight reals

PIED, variegated

PIE-POUDRES (Fr. pied-poudreux, dusty-foot), court held at fairs to administer justice to itinerant vendors and buyers

PILCHER, term of contempt; one who wore a buff or leather jerkin, as did the serjeants of the counter; a pilferer

PILED, pilled, peeled, bald

PILL'D, polled, fleeced

PIMLICO, "sometimes spoken of as a person—perhaps master of a house famous for a particular ale" (Gifford)

PINE, afflict, distress

PINK, stab with a weapon; pierce or cut in scallops for ornament

PINNACE, a go-between in infamous sense

PISMIRE, ant

PISTOLET, gold coin, worth about 6s.

PITCH, height of a bird of prey's flight

PLAGUE, punishment, torment

PLAIN, lament

PLAIN SONG, simple melody

PLAISE, plaice

PLANET, "struck with a—," planets were supposed to have powers of blasting or exercising secret influences

PLAUSIBLE, pleasing

PLAUSIBLY, approvingly

PLOT, plan

PLY, apply oneself to

POESIE, posy, motto inside a ring

POINT IN HIS DEVICE, exact in every particular

POINTE, tabbed laces or cords for fastening the breeches to the doublet

POINT-TRUSSER, one who trussed (tied) his master's points (q.v.)

POISE, weigh, balance

POKING-STICK, stick used for setting the plaits of ruffs

POLITIC, politician

POLITIC, judicious, prudent, political

POLITICIAN, plotter, intriguer

POLL, strip, plunder, gain by extortion

POMMANDER, ball of perfume, worn or hung about the person to prevent infection, or for foppery

POMMADO, vaulting on a horse without the aid of stirrups

PONTIC, sour

POPULAR, vulgar, of the populace

POPULOUS, numerous

PORT, gate; print of a deer's foot

PORT, transport

PORTAGUE, Portuguese gold coin, worth over £3 or f4

PORTCULLIS, "—of coin," some old coins have a portcullis stamped on their reverse (Whalley)

PORTENT, marvel, prodigy; sinister omen

PORTENTOUS, prophesying evil, threatening

PORTER, references appear "to allude to Parsons, the king's porter, who was . . . near seven feet high" (Whalley)

POSSESS, inform, acquaint

POST AND PAIR, a game at cards

POSY, motto. (See Poesie)

POTCH, poach

POULT-FOOT, club-foot

POUNCE, claw, talon

PRACTICE, intrigue, concerted plot

PRACTISE, plot, conspire

PRAGMATIC, an expert, agent

PRAGMATIC, officious, conceited, meddling

PRECEDENT, record of proceedings

PRECEPT, warrant, summons

PRECISIAN(ISM), Puritan(ism), preciseness

PREFER, recomment

PRESENCE, presence chamber

PRESENT(LY), immediate(ly), without delay; at the present time; actually

PRESS, force into service

PREST, ready

PRETEND, assert, allege

PREVENT, anticipate

PRICE, worth, excellence

PRICK, point, dot used in the writing of Hebrew and other languages

PRICK, prick out, mark off, select; trace, track; "—away," make off with speed

PRIMERO, game of cards

PRINCOX, pert boy

PRINT, "in—," to the letter, exactly

PRISTINATE, former

PRIVATE, private interests

PRIVATE, privy, intimate

PROCLIVE, prone to

PRODIGIOUS, monstrous, unnatural

PRODIGY, monster

PRODUCED, prolonged

PROFESS, pretend

PROJECTION, the throwing of the "powder of projection" into the crucible to turn the melted metal into gold or silver

PROLATE, pronounce drawlingly

PROPER, of good appearance, handsome; own, particular

PROPERTIES, state necessaries

PROPERTY, duty; tool

PRORUMPED, burst out

PROTEST, vow, proclaim (an affected word of that time); formally declare non-payment, etc., of bill of exchange; fig. failure of personal credit, etc.

PROVANT, soldier's allowance—hence, of common make

PROVIDE, foresee

PROVIDENCE, foresight, prudence

PUBLICATION, making a thing public of common property (N.E.D.)

PUCKFIST, puff-ball; insipid, insignificant, boasting fellow

PUFF-WING, shoulder puff

PUISNE, judge of inferior rank, a junior
PULCHRITUDE, beauty
PUMP, shoe
PUNGENT, piercing
PUNTO, point, hit
PURCEPT, precept, warrant
PURE, fine, capital, excellent
PURELY, perfectly, utterly
PURL, pleat or fold of a ruff
PURSE-NET, net of which the mouth is drawn together with a string
PURSUIVANT, state messenger who summoned the persecuted seminaries; warrant officer
PURSY, PURSINESS, shortwinded(ness)
PUT, make a push, exert yourself (N.E.D.)
PUT OFF, excuse, shift
PUT ON, incite, encourage; proceed with, take in hand, try

QUACKSALVER, quack
QUAINT, elegant, elaborated, ingenious, clever
QUAR, quarry
QUARRIED, seized, or fed upon, as prey
QUEAN, hussy, jade
QUEASY, hazardous, delicate
QUELL, kill, destroy
QUEST, request; inquiry
QUESTION, decision by force of arms
QUESTMAN, one appointed to make official inquiry
QUIB, QUIBLIN, quibble, quip
QUICK, the living
QUIDDIT, quiddity, legal subtlety
QUIRK, clever turn or trick
QUIT, requite, repay; acquit, absolve; rid; forsake, leave

QUITTER-BONE, disease of horses
QUODLING, codling
QUOIT, throw like a quoit, chuck
QUOTE, take note, observe, write down

RACK, neck of mutton or pork (Halliwell)
RAKE UP, cover over
RAMP, rear, as a lion, etc.
RAPT, carry away
RAPT, enraptured
RASCAL, young or inferior deer
RASH, strike with a glancing oblique blow, as a boar with its tusk
RATSEY, GOMALIEL, a famous highwayman
RAVEN, devour
REACH, understand
REAL, regal
REBATU, ruff, turned-down collar
RECTOR, RECTRESS, director, governor
REDARGUE, confute
REDUCE, bring back
REED, rede, counsel, advice
REEL, run riot
REFEL, refute
REFORMADOES, disgraced or disbanded soldiers
REGIMENT, government
REGRESSION, return
REGULAR ("Tale of a Tub"), regular noun (quibble) (N.E.D.)
RELIGION, "make—of," make a point of, scruple of
RELISH, savour
REMNANT, scrap of quotation
REMORA, species of fish
RENDER, depict, exhibit, show

REPAIR, reinstate

REPETITION, recital, narration

REREMOUSE, bat

RESIANT, resident

RESIDENCE, sediment

RESOLUTION, judgment, decision

RESOLVE, inform; assure; prepare, make up one's mind; dissolve; come to a decision, be convinced; relax, set at ease

RESPECTIVE, worthy of respect; regardful, discriminative

RESPECTIVELY, with reverence

RESPECTLESS, regardless

RESPIRE, exhale; inhale

RESPONSIBLE, correspondent

REST, musket-rest

REST, "set up one's—," venture one's all, one's last stake (from game of primero)

REST, arrest

RESTIVE, RESTY, dull, inactive

RETCHLESS(NESS), reckless(ness)

RETIRE, cause to retire

RETRICATO, fencing term

RETRIEVE, rediscovery of game once sprung

RETURNS, ventures sent abroad, for the safe return of which so much money is received

REVERBERATE, dissolve or blend by reflected heat

REVERSE, REVERSO, back-handed thrust, etc., in fencing

REVISE, reconsider a sentence

RHEUM, spleen, caprice

RIBIBE, abusive term for an old woman

RID, destroy, do away with

RIFLING, raffling, dicing

RING, "cracked within the—," coins so cracked were unfit for currency

RISSE, risen, rose
RIVELLED, wrinkled
ROARER, swaggerer
ROCHET, fish of the gurnet kind
ROCK, distaff
RODOMONTADO, braggadocio
ROGUE, vagrant, vagabond
RONDEL, "a round mark in the score of a public-house" (Nares); roundel
ROOK, sharper; fool, dupe
ROSAKER, similar to ratsbane
ROSA-SOLIS, a spiced spirituous liquor
ROSES, rosettes
ROUND, "gentlemen of the—," officers of inferior rank
ROUND TRUNKS, trunk hose, short loose breeches reaching almost or quite to the knees
ROUSE, carouse, bumper
ROVER, arrow used for shooting at a random mark at uncertain distance
ROWLY-POWLY, roly-poly
RUDE, RUDENESS, unpolished, rough(ness), coarse(ness)
RUFFLE, flaunt, swagger
RUG, coarse frieze
RUG-GOWNS, gown made of rug
RUSH, reference to rushes with which the floors were then strewn
RUSHER, one who strewed the floor with rushes
RUSSET, homespun cloth of neutral or reddish-brown colour

SACK, loose, flowing gown
SADLY, seriously, with gravity
SAD(NESS), sober, serious(ness)
SAFFI, bailiffs

ST. THOMAS A WATERINGS, place in Surrey where criminals were
    executed
SAKER, small piece of ordnance
SALT, leap
SALT, lascivious
SAMPSUCHINE, sweet marjoram
SARABAND, a slow dance
SATURNALS, began December 17
SAUCINESS, presumption, insolence
SAUCY, bold, impudent, wanton
SAUNA (Lat.), a gesture of contempt
SAVOUR, perceive; gratify, please; to partake of the nature
SAY, sample
SAY, assay, try
SCALD, word of contempt, implying dirt and disease
SCALLION, shalot, small onion
SCANDERBAG, "name which the Turks (in allusion to Alexander the
    Great) gave to the brave Castriot, chief of Albania, with whom
    they had continual wars. His romantic life had just been translated"
    (Gifford)
SCAPE, escape
SCARAB, beetle
SCARTOCCIO, fold of paper, cover, cartouch, cartridge
SCONCE, head
SCOPE, aim
SCOT AND LOT, tax, contribution (formerly a parish assessment)
SCOTOMY, dizziness in the head
SCOUR, purge
SCOURSE, deal, swap
SCRATCHES, disease of horses
SCROYLE, mean, rascally fellow
SCRUPLE, doubt

SEAL, put hand to the giving up of property or rights
SEALED, stamped as genuine
SEAM-RENT, ragged
SEAMING LACES, insertion or edging
SEAR UP, close by searing, burning
SEARCED, sifted
SECRETARY, able to keep a secret
SECULAR, worldly, ordinary, commonplace
SECURE, confident
SEELIE, happy, blest
SEISIN, legal term: possession
SELLARY, lewd person
SEMBLABLY, similarly
SEMINARY, a Romish priest educated in a foreign seminary
SENSELESS, insensible, without sense or feeling
SENSIBLY, perceptibly
SENSIVE, sensitive
SENSUAL, pertaining to the physical or material
SERENE, harmful dew of evening
SERICON, red tincture
SERVANT, lover
SERVICES, doughty deeds of arms
SESTERCE, Roman copper coin
SET, stake, wager
SET UP, drill
SETS, deep plaits of the ruff
SEWER, officer who served up the feast, and brought water for the
    hands of the guests
SHAPE, a suit by way of disguise
SHIFT, fraud, dodge
SHIFTER, cheat
SHITTLE, shuttle; "shittle-cock," shuttlecock

SHOT, tavern reckoning

SHOT-CLOG, one only tolerated because he paid the shot (reckoning) for the rest

SHOT-FREE, scot-free, not having to pay

SHOVE-GROAT, low kind of gambling amusement, perhaps somewhat of the nature of pitch and toss

SHOT-SHARKS, drawers

SHREWD, mischievous, malicious, curst

SHREWDLY, keenly, in a high degree

SHRIVE, sheriff; posts were set up before his door for proclamations, or to indicate his residence

SHROVING, Shrovetide, season of merriment

SIGILLA, seal, mark

SILENCED BRETHERN, MINISTERS, those of the Church or Nonconformists who had been silenced, deprived, etc.

SILLY, simple, harmless

SIMPLE, silly, witless; plain, true

SIMPLES, herbs

SINGLE, term of chase, signifying when the hunted stag is separated from the herd, or forced to break covert

SINGLE, weak, silly

SINGLE-MONEY, small change

SINGULAR, unique, supreme

SI-QUIS, bill, advertisement

SKELDRING, getting money under false pretences; swindlilng

SKILL, "it—a not," matters not

SEINK(ER), pour, draw(er), tapster

SKIRT, tail

SLEEK, smooth

SLICE, fire shovel or pan (dial.)

SLICK, sleek, smooth

'SLID, 'SLIGHT, 'SPRECIOUS, irreverent oaths

SLIGHT, sleight, cunning, cleverness; trick

SLIP, counterfeit coin, bastard

SLIPPERY, polished and shining

SLOPS, large loose breeches

SLOT, print of a stag's foot

SLUR, put a slur on; chear (by sliding a die in some way)

SMELT, gull, simpleton

SNORLE, "perhaps snarl as Puppy is addressed" (Cunningham)

SNOTTERIE, filth

SNUFF, anger, resentment; "take in—," take offence at

SNUFFERS, small open silver dishes for holding snuff, or receptacle for
     placing snuffers in (Halliwell)

SOCK, shoe worn by comic actors

SOD, seethe

SOGGY, soaked, sodden

SOIL, "take—," said of a hunted stag when he takes to the water for
     safety

SOL, sou

SOLDADOES, soldiers

SOLICIT, rouse, excite to action

SOOTH, flattery, cajolery

SOOTHE, flatter, humour

SOPHISTICATE, adulterate

SORT, company, party; rank, degree

SORT, suit, fit; select

SOUSE, ear

SOUSED ("Devil is an Ass"), fol. read "sou't," which Dyce interprets as
     "a variety of the spelling of 'shu'd': to shu is to scare a bird away."
     (See his Webster, p. 350)

SOWTER, cobbler

SPAGYRICA, chemistry according to the teachings of Paracelsus

SPAR, bar

SPEAK, make known, proclaim
SPECULATION, power of sight
SPED, to have fared well, prospered
SPEECE, species
SPIGHT, anger, rancour
SPINNER, spider
SPINSTRY, lewd person
SPITTLE, hospital, lazar-house
SPLEEN, considered the seat of the emotions
SPLEEN, caprice, humour, mood
SPRUNT, spruce
SPURGE, foam
SPUR-RYAL, gold coin worth 15s.
SQUIRE, square, measure; "by the—," exactly.
STAGGERING, wavering, hesitating
STAIN, disparagement, disgrace
STALE, decoy, or cover, stalking-horse
STALE, make cheap, common
STALE, approach stealthily or under cover
STALL, forestall
STANDARD, suit
STAPLE, market emporium
STARK, downright
STARTING-HOLES, loopholes of escape
STATE, dignity; canopied chair of state; estate
STATUMINATE, support vines by poles or stakes; used by Pliny
    (Gifford)
STAY, gag
STAY, await; detain
STICKLER, second or umpire
STIGMATISE, mark, brand
STILL, continual(ly), constant(ly)

228

STINKARD, stinking fellow

STINT, stop

STIPTIC, astringent

STOCCATA, thrust in fencing

STOCK-FISH, salted and dried fish

STOMACH, pride, valour

STOMACH, resent

STOOP, swoop down as a hawk

STOP, fill, stuff

STOPPLE, stopper

STOTE, stoat, weasel

STOUP, stoop, swoop=bow

STRAIGHT, straightway

STRAMAZOUN (Ital. stramazzone), a down blow, as opposed to the thrust

STRANGE, like a stranger, unfamiliar

STRANGENESS, distance of behaviour

STREIGHTS, OR BERMUDAS, labyrinth of alleys and courts in the Strand

STRIGONIUM, Grau in Hungary, taken from the Turks in 1597

STRIKE, balance (accounts)

STRINGHALT, disease of horses

STROKER, smoother, flatterer

STROOK, p.p. of "strike"

STRUMMEL-PATCHED, strummed is glossed in dialect dicts. as "a long, loose and dishevelled head of hair"

STUDIES, studious efforts

STYLE, title; pointed instrument used for writing on wax tablets

SUBTLE, fine, delicate, thin; smooth, soft

SUBTLETY (SUBTILITY), subtle device

SUBURB, connected with loose living

SUCCUBAE, demons in form of women

SUCK, extract money from

SUFFERANCE, suffering

SUMMED, term of falconry: with full-grown plumage

SUPER-NEGULUM, topers turned the cup bottom up when it was empty

SUPERSTITIOUS, over-scrupulous

SUPPLE, to make pliant

SURBATE, make sore with walking

SURCEASE, cease

SUR-REVERENCE, save your reverence

SURVISE, peruse

SUSCITABILITY, excitability

SUSPECT, suspicion

SUSPEND, suspect

SUSPENDED, held over for the present

SUTLER, victualler

SWAD, clown, boor

SWATH BANDS, swaddling clothes

SWINGE, beat

TABERD, emblazoned mantle or tunic worn by knights and heralds

TABLE(S), "pair of—," tablets, note-book

TABOR, small drum

TABRET, tabor

TAFFETA, silk; "tuft-taffeta," a more costly silken fabric

TAINT, "—a staff," break a lance at tilting in an unscientific or dishonourable manner

TAKE IN, capture, subdue

TAKE ME WITH YOU, let me understand you

TAKE UP, obtain on credit, borrow

TALENT, sum or weight of Greek currency

TALL, stout, brave

TANKARD-BEARERS, men employed to fetch water from the conduits

TARLETON, celebrated comedian and jester

TARTAROUS, like a Tartar

TAVERN-TOKEN, "to swallow a—," get drunk

TELL, count

TELL-TROTH, truth-teller

TEMPER, modify, soften

TENDER, show regard, care for cherish; manifest

TENT, "take—," take heed

TERSE, swept and polished

TERTIA, "that portion of an army levied out of one particular district or division of a country" (Gifford)

TESTON, tester, coin worth 6d.

THIRDBOROUGH, constable

THREAD, quality

THREAVES, droves

THREE-FARTHINGS, piece of silver current under Elizabeth

THREE-PILED, of finest quality, exaggerated

THRIFTILY, carefully

THRUMS, ends of the weaver's warp; coarse yarn made from

THUMB-RING, familiar spirits were supposed capable of being carried about in various ornaments or parts of dress

TIBICINE, player on the tibia, or pipe

TICK-TACK, game similar to backgammon

TIGHTLY, promptly

TIM, (?) expressive of a climax of nonentity

TIMELESS, untimely, unseasonable

TINCTURE, an essential or spiritual principle supposed by alchemists to be transfusible into material things; an imparted characteristic or tendency

TINK, tinkle

TIPPET, "turn—," change behaviour or way of life

TIPSTAFF, staff tipped with metal

TIRE, head-dress

TIRE, feed ravenously, like a bird of prey

TITILLATION, that which tickles the senses, as a perfume

TOD, fox

TOILED, worn out, harassed

TOKEN, piece of base metal used in place of very small coin, when this was scarce

TONNELS, nostrils

TOP, "parish—," large top kept in villages for amusement and exercise in frosty weather when people were out of work

TOTER, tooter, player on a wind instrument

TOUSE, pull, read

TOWARD, docile, apt; on the way to; as regards; present, at hand

TOY, whim; trick; term of contempt

TRACT, attraction

TRAIN, allure, entice

TRANSITORY, transmittable

TRANSLATE, transform

TRAY-TRIP, game at dice (success depended on throwing a three) (Nares)

TREACHOUR (TRECHER), traitor

TREEN, wooden

TRENCHER, serving-man who carved or served food

TRENDLE-TAIL, trundle-tail, curly-tailed

TRICK (TRICKING), term of heraldry: to draw outline of coat of arms, etc., without blazoning

TRIG, a spruce, dandified man

TRILL, trickle

TRILLIBUB, tripe, any worthless, trifling thing

TRIPOLY, "come from—," able to perform feats of agility, a "jest nominal," depending on the first part of the word (Gifford)

232

TRITE, worn, shabby
TRIVIA, three-faced goddess (Hecate)
TROJAN, familiar term for an equal or inferior; thief
TROLL, sing loudly
TROMP, trump, deceive
TROPE, figure of speech
TROW, think, believe, wonder
TROWLE, troll
TROWSES, breeches, drawers
TRUCHMAN, interpreter
TRUNDLE, JOHN, well-known printer
TRUNDLE, roll, go rolling along
TRUNDLING CHEATS, term among gipsies and beggars for carts or
    coaches (Gifford)
TRUNK, speaking-tube
TRUSS, tie the tagged laces that fastened the breeches to the doublet
TUBICINE, trumpeter
TUCKET (Ital. toccato), introductory flourish on the trumpet
TUITION, guardianship
TUMBLE, a particular kind of dog so called from the mode of his
    hunting
TUMBREL-SLOP, loose, baggy breeches
TURD, excrement
TUSK, gnash the teeth (Century Dict.)
TWIRE, peep, twinkle
TWOPENNY ROOM, gallery
TYRING-HOUSE, attiring-room

ULENSPIEGEL. See Howleglass
UMBRATILE, like or pertaining to a shadow
UMBRE, brown dye
UNBATED, unabated

UNBORED, (?) excessively bored

UNCARNATE, not fleshly, or of flesh

UNCOUTH, strange, unusual

UNDERTAKER, "one who undertook by his influence in the House of Commons to carry things agreeably to his Majesty's wishes" (Whalley); one who becomes surety for

UNEQUAL, unjust

UNEXCEPTED, no objection taken at

UNFEARED, unaffrighted

UNHAPPILY, unfortunately

UNICORN'S HORN, supposed antidote to poison

UNKIND(LY), unnatural(ly)

UNMANNED, untamed (term in falconry)

UNQUIT, undischarged

UNREADY, undressed

UNRUDE, rude to an extreme

UNSEASONED, unseasonable, unripe

UNSEELED, a hawk's eyes were "seeled" by sewing the eyelids together with fine thread

UNTIMELY, unseasonably

UNVALUABLE, invaluable

UPBRAID, make a matter of reproach

UPSEE, heavy kind of Dutch beer (Halliwell); "—Dutch," in the Dutch fashion

UPTAILS ALL, refrain of a popular song

URGE, allege as accomplice, instigator

URSHIN, URCHIN, hedgehog

USE, interest on money; part of sermon dealing with the practical application of doctrine

USE, be in the habit of, accustomed to; put out to interest

USQUEBAUGH, whisky

USURE, usury

234

UTTER, put in circulation, make to pass current; put forth for sale

VAIL, bow, do homage
VAILS, tips, gratuities
VALL. See Vail
VALLIES (Fr. valise), portmanteau, bag
VAPOUR(S) (n. and v.), used affectedly, like "humour," in many senses, often very vaguely and freely ridiculed by Jonson; humour, disposition, whims, brag(ging), hector(ing), etc.
VARLET, bailiff, or serjeant-at-mace
VAUT, vault
VEER (naut.), pay out
VEGETAL, vegetable; person full of life and vigour
VELLUTE, velvet
VELVET CUSTARD. Cf. "Taming of the Shrew," iv. 3, 82, "custard coffin," coffin being the raised crust over a pie
VENT, vend, sell; give outlet to; scent snuff up
VENUE, bout (fencing term)
VERDUGO (Span.), hangman, executioner
VERGE, "in the—," within a certain distance of the court
VEX, agitate, torment
VICE, the buffoon of old moralities; some kind of machinery for moving a puppet (Gifford)
VIE AND REVIE, to hazard a certain sum, and to cover it with a larger one.

VINCENT AGAINST YORK, two heralds-at-arms
VINDICATE, avenge
VIRGE, wand, rod
VIRGINAL, old form of piano
VIRTUE, valour
VIVELY, in lifelike manner, livelily

VIZARD, mask
VOGUE, rumour, gossip
VOICE, vote
VOID, leave, quit
VOLARY, cage, aviary
VOLLEY, "at—," "o' the volee," at random (from a term of tennis)
VORLOFFE, furlough

WADLOE, keeper of the Devil Tavern, where Jonson and his friends
    met in the 'Apollo' room (Whalley)
WAIGHTS, waits, night musicians, "band of musical watchmen"
    (Webster), or old form of "hautboys"
WANNION, "vengeance," "plague" (Nares)
WARD, a famous pirate
WARD, guard in fencing
WATCHET, pale, sky blue
WEAL, welfare
WEED, garment
WEFT, waif
WEIGHTS, "to the gold—," to every minute particular
WELKIN, sky
WELL-SPOKEN, of fair speech
WELL-TORNED, turned and polished, as on a wheel
WELT, hem, border of fur
WHER, whether
WHETSTONE, GEORGE, an author who lived 1544(?) to 1587(?)
WHIFF, a smoke, or drink; "taking the—," inhaling the tobacco smoke
    or some such accomplishment
WHIGH-HIES, neighings, whinnyings
WHIMSY, whim, "humour"
WHINILING, (?) whining, weakly
WHIT, (?) a mere jot

WHITEMEAT, food made of milk or eggs

WICKED, bad, clumsy

WICKER, pliant, agile

WILDING, esp. fruit of wild apple or crab tree (Webster)

WINE, "I have the—for you," Prov.: I have the perquisites (of the office) which you are to share (Cunningham)

WINNY, "same as old word 'wonne', to stay, etc." (Whalley)

WISE-WOMAN, fortune-teller

WISH, recommend

WISS (WUSSE), "I—," certainly, of a truth

WITHHOUT, beyond

WITTY, cunning, ingenious, clever

WOOD, collection, lot

WOODCOCK, term of contempt

WOOLSACK ("—pies"), name of tavern

WORT, unfermented beer

WOUNDY, great, extreme

WREAK, revenge

WROUGHT, wrought upon

WUSSE, interjection. (See Wiss)

YEANLING, lamb, kid

ZANY, an inferior clown, who attended upon the chief fool and mimicked his tricks

Lightning Source UK Ltd.
Milton Keynes UK
UKHW022327060223
416579UK00001B/216